TO THE ~~████████~~ FAMILY.

It is my pleasure to dedicate this book to you. It includes some of the projects we did together, which lead to a wonderful friendship.

Signature

14-4-2011.

GREENARCHITECTURE.COM

JAVIER BARBA

GREENARCHITECTURE.COM

JAVIER BARBA

LOFT

GREENARCHITECTURE.COM

BC Estudio de Arquitectura
Plaza Equilaz, 10, ent. 3ª
08017 Barcelona, Spain
T +34 93 204 42 06
F +34 93 204 26 97
javbarba@bcarquitectos.com
www.greenarchitecture.com
www.bcarquitectos.com

Design and layout: **Mireia Casanovas Soley** // Edition and texts: **Aitana Lleonart** // Translation: **Cillero & de Motta**

© 2011 Loft Publications // Loft Publications, S. L. // Via Laietana, 32, 4°, of. 92 // 08003 Barcelona, Spain // Tel.: +34 932 688 088 // Fax: +34 932 687 073 // loft@loftpublications.com // www.loftpublications.com // ISBN: 978-84-92463-58-9 // Printed in Spain // All rights reserved. No part of this publication may be reproduced, stored in a retrieval sytem, or transmitted in any form or by any means, electronic, mechanical, photocopying, recording, or otherwise, without prior consent of the publishers.

6	**PREFACE**	
	SINGLE FAMILY DETACHED HOME	
12	RIERA HOUSE	Spain
18	MONJO HOUSE	Spain
26	CARALPS HOUSE	Spain
28	SEMEL HOUSE	Spain
30	MORA HOUSE	Spain
34	GIRÓ SUMMER PAVILION	Spain
38	MORA HOUSE	Spain
42	ZERMOMA HOUSE	Spain
48	BARBA HOUSE	Spain
56	PI SUNYER HOUSE	Spain
60	IRBESAMA HOUSE	Spain
64	TUSQUETS HOUSE	Spain
72	LORD ROTHSCHILD SUMMER PAVILION	Greece
82	TSIRIGAKIS HOUSE	Greece
92	DELIGIANNIS HOUSE	Greece
98	KOKKALIS HOUSE	Greece
106	PAMEKAS HOUSE	Greece
114	ECONOMOU – VOSNIADES HOUSES	Greece
120	TERZOPOULOS HOUSE	Greece
124	RALLIS HOUSE	Greece
130	PARASCHIS HOUSE	Greece
132	DUNMOW HOUSE	Greece
134	KANTARZOPOULOS HOUSE	Greece
136	HOUSE IN RODOPOLI	Greece
138	VAN VEGGEL HOUSE	Portugal
142	CHALETS IN PINHAL VELHO	Portugal
146	GREENLANDIA	Russia
148	APARTMENT IN ST. PETERSBURG	Russia
150	HUNEEUS HOUSE	USA
152	GIROD HOUSE	Mexico
	RESIDENTIAL COMPLEXES	
154	LA ISLA VERDE ©	Spain
160	PREDIO DE SA FÚA	Spain
166	18 HOUSES IN AIGUABLAVA	Spain
170	VILLAGE IN SANT MORI	Spain
172	VILLAGE ON PAROS ISLAND	Greece
174	HOUSES IN LIA	Greece
176	BLACK STONE	Greece
178	HRH PRINCE SULTAN BIN FAHAD RED SEA RESIDENCE	Saudi Arabia
	HOTELS	
182	LUXURY RESORT HOTEL IN BOROBUDUR	Indonesia
184	SAN BLAS VALLEY RESORT	Spain
186	CONDOHOTEL MOJÁCAR FOR GROUP MED	Spain
188	SAN BASILIO HOTEL RESORT	Mexico
192	THERAPEUTIC-TOURISM COMPLEX	Spain
194	OUED BOUTIQUE HOTEL ©	Morocco
	SPORTS AND LEISURE FACILITIES	
196	GREEN UNDER GREEN	Spain
200	RCD ESPANYOL SHOPPING MALL	Spain
204	ALICE IN WONDERLAND. KRISTIANSAND PERFORMING ARTS CENTER	Norway
206	CLUB HOUSE. GOLF LA GRAIERA	Spain
210	CLUB HOUSE AND SPA IN POLAND	Poland
	WINERIES	
216	STAG'S LEAP WINE CELLARS	USA
222	STAG'S LEAP WINE CELLARS VISITOR CENTER	USA
224	INTERVENTION IN SOTO DE TORRES FOR BODEGAS TORRES	Spain
226	WALTRAUD CELLAR FOR BODEGAS TORRES	Spain
	OTHER PROJECTS	
236	HRH PRINCE SULTAN BIN FAHAD RESIDENCE IN CANNES	France
238	COLONQUES HOUSE	Spain
239	SWAROVSKI HOUSE	Spain
240	CHILE-CALIFORNIA ROOM FOR BODEGAS TORRES	Spain
241	FORUM MONTIJO	Portugal
242	LANDSCAPE IN VALLSOLANA	Spain
243	PIOLETS HOTEL	Andorra
244	PÉREZ DEL PULGAR HOUSE	Spain
245	GARCÍA NIETO HOUSE	Spain
246	PLANELLS HOUSE	Spain
247	FERRER HOUSE	Spain
248	SÁNCHEZ VICARIO HOUSE	Spain
249	ALMADA FORUM	Portugal
250	**WORKS AND PROJECTS**	
255	**ESTUDIO BC**	
256	**PUBLICATIONS LIST**	

THE BARBAS, A DYNASTY OF ARCHITECTS

Javier Barba belongs to the fourth generation of a dynasty of Catalan architects that began with his great-great grandfather, Francisco Barba Masip, who was one of the favorite students of Antoni Celles, professor emeritus at La Llotja, the first school of architecture in Barcelona. This school standardized the use of the neoclassic style as a compositional framework for solving the inherent problems of architectural projects at a time when measures were being taken to improve and professionalize the guild structure that had prevailed since the Middle Ages. Francisco Barba Masip subsequently became the architect for the province of Tarragona and one of those in charge of refurbishing Poblet Monastery, as well as designing several buildings in a neoclassic style.
(Photos 1, 2, 3)

Javier's grandfather was the architect and builder Alfonso Barba Miracle, who designed several buildings in an Art Nouveau or eclectic style, many of which are located in the Eixample district of Barcelona. (Photos 4, 5, 6)

He is also the son of another architect, Francisco Juan Barba Corsini, one of the most prominent members of the modern movement in Spain. He had firsthand knowledge of the conflict with neoclassical precepts experienced by his father, who suffered a creative crisis, after watching the movie *The Fountainhead* directed by King Vidor. This led him to abandon his books on academic architecture and to embrace modern architecture, bequeathing such prominent works for historiography as the apartments of La Pedrera and the Mitre Building. Finally, Javier Barba is the father of yet another architect, Gabriel Barba. His library houses all the books accumulated as a result of his family's architectural practice for more than 150 years.
(Photos 7, 8, 9)

CONTEXT OF A UNIQUE WORK

The modern movement is an international trend that emerged from the first wave of the European avant-garde at the beginning of the 20th century and spread considerably during the 1920s. Despite its richness and complexity, it clearly laid the foundations for a number of concepts, attitudes and forms: a functionalist defense of the prominence of the human race; the use of a creative system in which method and reason are crucial; the confidence that new technological resources were transforming the human stage in a positive way; and an emphasis on the social value of architecture. Its crucial, transforming momentum contained the legitimating principles for a new social order based on productive and technological rationality.

Architecture, which is a discipline that is sensitive both to artistic phenomena and also to their technical and productive equivalents, soon harnessed all its imagination in pursuit of this new perspective. More metaphors for the new order were constructed than spaces in which to live. Criticism and dissemination of modern architecture, not far removed from its very evolution, eventually served to categorize this phenomenon. Thus, the quest for a new architectural synthesis in keeping with social, cultural and technical innovations, along with efforts to find a «utopian» dimension to the new humanistic ideals of the emerging architecture, were reduced to the category of style, even if it was internationally and universally valid.

Nevertheless, such a revolutionary form of new language was subject to certain assumptions that afforded prominence to men and women, turning a blind eye to the importance of the natural surroundings. In much of the work produced by the modern movement an attempt is made to suggest an unwitting association between form and policy from an esthetic point of view. Thus, the transparency of the façades, achieved with the independent structure made up of glass walls, can be equated with honesty; the open plan with democracy and the broad range of choice; and the absence of ornamentation with economy and ethical integrity.

What predominates during the second half of the 20th century is an immense panorama of continuations, developments, reviews and criticism, with respect to this type of dead point, which represented the experience of the avant-garde. Postmodern artists subsequently

Francisco Barba Masip (1815-1890)

1. Gasset House, Tarragona, 1859

2. Tarragona City Hall, 1862-1865

3. Joan Gatell i Badia House, Tarragona

Alfonso Barba Miracle (1898-1960)

4. Rabadà House, Tarragona, 1918

5. Bartolomé Trias House, Barcelona, 1921

6. Tomàs Mallol House, Eixample Barcelona

Francisco Juan Barba Corsini (1916-2008)

7. Mitre Building, Barcelona, 1958-1963

8. Apartments of La Pedrera, Barcelona, 1953-1955

9. Pérez del Pulgar Chalet, Cadaqués, 1958

Photos © Català Roca

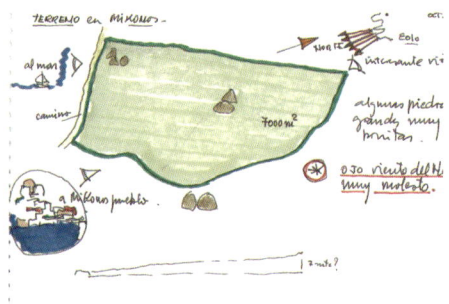

10. Tsigirakis House, Mykonos (Greece), 1997

11. Sketch Lord J. Rothschild Summer Pavilion, Corfu (Greece)

12. Lord Rothschild Summer Pavilion, Corfu (Greece), 1993

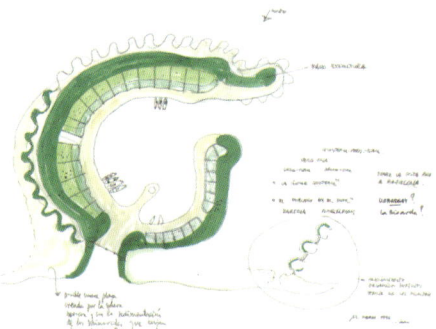

La Isla Verde©, Barcelona (Spain), 1992

decided to bring other fringe identities to light, particularly those of an environmental nature.

PROJECT METHODOLOGY AND ITS APPLICATION

Apart from knowledge, the brain can also store new experiences. When we try something, our sensory nerves transmit vast amounts of information to the brain about what we are seeing, smelling, tasting, hearing and feeling. In response, the neurons in the brain divide up into networks of connections reflecting the experience. These neurons also release chemical substances that trigger certain sensations. Each new experience gives rise to a feeling.

These assumptions form the starting point for the projects devised by architect Javier Barba, which appear to be extensions of the environment. Experiencing the peculiarities of the scenery and the land *in situ* are what creates the experience, and in turn defines the project. Inspiration is triggered by the new experience like a seed germinating subsequent development in the design, which in turn takes into account the role to be filled by the building and the human needs of its future occupants. Referring to the rugged terrain, Barba says: "When you see a rock, don't remove it. It is giving you information about how to begin the project." The geographic and geometric constraints inspired by vernacular forms represent the basis of the project.
(Photo 10)

Thus, in order to capture the experience, Javier Barba thinks the best thing to do is to visit the site at different times of the day: from dawn to dusk, exploring and capturing the holistic sense of the area. In light of his opinion, the "best thing" would be to experience it, not merely in the course of a single day, but during the four seasons of the year so as to be able to extract, from each of these, the feelings and sensations captured from the energy that has been fused in time and space.

The ideas triggered by such inspiration are sketched out right there on the spot. It is not a question of divine inspiration, but rather the fact that, as the architect, Josef Hoffman (Czech Republic, 1870–1956) wrote to his friend Oscar Kokoschka, "intelligence and boundless knowledge can kill cultural momentum. The only thing that counts is adequate perception and innate sensitivity." This notion might be applied to Javier Barba, who, far from imitating his contemporaries and the architecture currently being produced, generates his design on the basis of his own inner being and in harmony with nature itself. Not everyone has the capacity and sensitivity to recognize and capture "powerful" places defined by nature itself, with its vegetation, trees and huge rocks.
(Photo 11)

This gives rise to the functional scheme. Nowadays, studying the local environment is generally neglected, and houses are planned without any attention to the natural environment, which causes an unnecessary waste of energy. In contrast, Javier Barba's projects take orientation into consideration, which offers bioclimatic designs that are powered by the best solar energy and optimize natural ventilation. Bioclimatic architecture, which he defines as a bridge between people and nature rather than a style, respects nature and its resources, offering the occupants the most comfortable and pleasant atmosphere possible.

Taken as a whole – with photographs of the site, sketches and form drawings – the design gradually takes shape. In the words of architect Louis Kahn, "it is not a question of design preceding form, because the latter is unchanging and tied to the idea of a house." The design is altered in keeping with the local topography, the idiosyncrasies of the climate, the light available and, of course, the needs of the occupant. "An architect must be like a good actor who adapts to different roles," he adds. Architecture does not merely entail covering the areas prescribed by the client. The creation of spaces should evoke the feeling that it is being used properly.

Hence, the design is also influenced by the client's needs. The architect has to have the sensitivity and ability to interpret the client's wishes and think about the design, based on this and all the factors explained above. He has to decide on what is most likely to meet with their approval – deciding whether to make it stimulating or more relaxing. As Barba says, "it is a very slow

process, discussing feelings, walking over the site, making sketches and models."
(Photo 12)

Barba is very meticulous and attentive to detail, so that the swimming pool becomes a key element in the overall design. When the project is to be built on a cliff, the pool is always positioned on its edge, offering a panoramic effect on the horizon, as if it were a vantage point over the sea, blurring the boundaries between them. Waterfalls are also added to the project tripping over the rocks and flowing into the pool itself.

DESIGNING WITH NATURE

Most designers tend to draw the locations for their projects as if they were a separate item, making a distinction between architecture and nature. Both within and between ecosystems, there is a network of mutual dependence, so that changes occurring in part of the system affect the functioning of the whole, even when the degree of dependence may seem somewhat remote. Given the inseparability of the interaction between ecosystems, Javier Barba does not offer a fragmentary point of view.

The Barcelona architect analyzes each location for the various projects on an individual basis, because each site has its own ecological features and landscape. In fact, each system has its own physical structure and its own interactions. Not satisfied with adopting a simplistic approach to the project or endowing it with a single aim, the concept for the project is conceived within the overall context of the ecosystem operating as a whole.
(Photo 13)

For Javier Barba, locations are not all the same. Each one is assessed individually, depending on the natural values typical of its ecosystem, its processes, limitations, and inherent range of natural opportunities.

Barba's buildings are erected on the site in harmony with the landscape. The architect has dug into hillsides and taken advantage of quarries and rocks to shelter his houses, so as to reduce energy and blur the boundaries between architecture and landscape.

Thus, he uses the natural opportunities the ecosystem has to offer. The green cover may help to reduce extreme temperatures, filter dust, provide protection from the wind and maintain the appropriate amount of humidity in the area.

This is precisely why it is so important for him to keep the vegetation in every project, even when the building is located in a more developed area. In fact, some of his projects, such as the Riera House in Sant Andreu de Llavaneras or the Giró Summer Pavilion have roof gardens that help integrate the building into the landscape and provide efficient thermal and acoustic insulation.
(Photos 14, 15)

Light is an extremely important element in architecture. Good natural lighting in a house does not only solve energy problems, but also offers decorative appeal, bestowing the place with atmosphere. For this reason, care is taken to give the houses in Barba's projects the right orientation. As Le Corbusier said, "architecture is the encounter between light and form," but this architecture should not disrupt the peace and beauty of the place.

Hence, his projects include a holistic, comprehensive approach to the management of energy resources and materials for the structures, since his mission is to produce simple, green designs, applying this criterion not only to the elite residences of his select clients, but to any type of building.
(Photo 16)

DIVERSITY OF ARCHITECTURAL VOCABULARY

Unlike the great Swiss architect Le Corbusier, who defined the five points for a new school of architecture by building a number of so-called "purist" villas, Javier Barba does not possess a clearly encoded vocabulary, since each project is erected in a different place. Even so, certain themes do indeed recur in his houses: a hall in the entrance separating the busiest rooms from the sleeping areas; indoor and outdoor living areas; natural

13. Entrance of Riera House, Sant Andreu de Llavaneras (Spain), 1986

14. Riera House, Sant Andreu de Llavaneras (Spain), 1986

15. Giró Summer Pavilion, Sitges (Spain), 1995

16. 18 Houses in Aiguablava. (Spain), 2003

17. Monjo House, Cala Pregonda, Minorca (Spain), 1990

18. Tsirigakis House, Mykonos (Greece), 1997

19. Girod House, Baja California (Mexico), 2000

20. Barba House, Delta de l'Ebre (Spain), 2000

stone used together with concrete in earthy tones; or circular pavilions that shade a terrace dining area from the sun. There is also generally a marked geometry that is softened by the cladding on the outer walls, features determined by the Mediterranean climate, and the owners' wish to escape from the routine of city life and live closer to nature.

Thus, it is not the same thing to build a house in a woodland area on the Costa Brava as one perched on a rocky outcrop in a cove in Minorca, in the highlands on the island of Mykonos, or the environs of Baja California. Although all the projects are based on vernacular geometric forms, each location has its own characteristics, determined by the lie of the land, or by the climate in general, etc.
(Photos 17, 18, 19)

The images seen above are a good example of this. There is a clear relationship between form and appearance. The difference is that one house is perched on a cliff while the other has been erected on the flat surface of the land, which is likely to lead to a slight variation in building technique or use of materials. In Barba House, the stone cladding on the house is an attempt at camouflage and complicity.
(Photo 20)

The initial forms are determined by the lie of the land; the materials used for construction are native and therefore naturally more resistant to local weather conditions; and the color, which is "key to maintaining unity," says Barba, integrates with the natural surroundings.

If we *flashback* to the 1920s, we recall the De Stijl movement and neoplasticism, an artistic vein that is limited to basic elements – planes and lines, vertical and horizontal, primary colors (red, yellow and blue) and non-colors (black, white, gray), the best example of which is Shroder House by Gerrit Rietveld. It is precisely these three primary colors, according to Barba, which should never be used in architecture. Moreover, the neoplastic utopia aims to move architecture and man away from nature: "The more mature humanity becomes, [...] the more opposed to physical nature and the natural environment it will be [...]. People will therefore not miss the absence of natural scenery [...]. Human beings that have truly evolved will no longer seek to reorganize, shelter or embellish with flowers or trees [...]". Their utopian, transcendental philosophy has absolutely nothing to do with Barba's architecture.

His designs shun all ostentation, preferring a quiet location, as the architecture is not intended to be extravagant to create an impression but comfortable and emotionally satisfying, with its simple lines inspired in vernacular forms. Barba's architecture detaches itself from fashion, and is instead developed by tradition and necessity.

THE WHOLE ENSEMBLE IS TRIGGERED BY FEELING

Thus, in accordance with the criteria explained above, in De Stijl's projects, the building technique – the functional role and formal composition, or structure, form and function, which basically amounts to the same thing – are united under the concept of design. However, this concept (which was the result of what was already brewing in the early 20th century, fueled by the theories of Viollet le Duc or the Arts&Crafts) caught on and was developed further at the Bauhaus. The early beginnings of this German school have exerted a huge influence on all areas of design until our time, not only due to the force of their ideas, but also because of their style. In architecture, the most obvious example is white cubic house architecture, which is based on the search for economy, rationality and maximum functionality, and is consequently often described as cold, a superficial and intuitive criticism, which nevertheless responds to one of the key issues of contemporary esthetic experience. Houses which, unlike those designed by Barba, have absolutely nothing to do with their environment.

For Javier Barba, no emotion means the design is no good. This should be triggered by feeling, much like a reflection, regarding the natural environment, and not the product of technical reproduction and standardization, always based on the same principles. "Technique is not the most important thing. What we need to understand is the energy of life, to seek out the soul, to understand the role of feeling and individuality. In architecture, it is clear that technique is merely an aid, but not a definitive, separate phenomenon by itself. Technical functionality cannot define architecture," according to Alvar Aalto.

The optimum design integrates human beings and nature in accordance with ethical principles. Barba identifies with the following reflection extracted from an issue of the American magazine *Architectural Digest*: "Good design moves people because it offers something out of the ordinary, it is intelligence made tangible. Adherence to excellence." That is to say, good design is no longer just structure, form and function. Instead, the project method has to encompass the technical aspects and also the human and natural side as well. As the architect Louis Kahn said, "Beauty comes from selection. Affinities, integration, love."
(Photo 21)

It is obvious that a building needs to be practical and functional; otherwise it would have no sense. However, if that sense were all it had, then we would forget that places and spaces are also communicative: they transmit a given energy. This is a type of unwitting communication, which conditions the way we behave and see things, without our realizing it.

COMMUNICATION OF THE PROJECT

"We spend our lives chasing after an optimum state of mind, an idea of ourselves that we find pleasing. It is a very personal hunt, with the goal being understood by each person in his own way. However, without realizing it, practically all of us go searching for happiness a long way away without seeing that, in most cases, what really makes us happy is usually much closer than we think." It is clear that this paragraph taken from *The Architecture of Happiness* by Alain de Botton links up with the architectural philosophy espoused by Barba. It is precisely the physical environment that is of such paramount importance. We often forget that a huge machine capable of generating happiness or unhappiness (depending on the way each person sees it) is the physical space that surrounds us: the good or bad design of the streets we walk along, or the usefulness and beauty of the furniture we use are full of connotations arousing this or that emotion in us.

In the house-building process, there are several people involved (the client, the architect, the builder, etc.), and these people's values are imprinted on it in one way or another. In the home, the most important thing is how we live, but if the building has been erected using highly sterilized methods, it will be really difficult for it to transmit positive energy. The term 'sterilized' makes us think of all the new buildings that have been erected en masse over the past few years thanks to the *boom* in the property market, a subject that is not really relevant but links up with Barba's standpoint regarding the bad design of most of the buildings around us. As far as he is concerned, if he had to build in the city, the buildings would be as self-sufficient as possible: with roof gardens, solar panels and window boxes on the façades.

My intention is none other than to relate what I have said above to one of Javier Barba's main aims: finding comfortable atmospheres for the inhabitants of the designed space. A design that aims to harmonize architecture and landscape in keeping with people's feelings to enable them to achieve inner wellbeing. With respect to the environment, Barba believes that the more appropriate the site is, the happier the client will be.

NOTHING COMES OUT OF NOTHING

It is evident that, like every other architect, in order to get this far, Javier Barba has had his own sources of reference. Among these, and the most important of them all, is the American architect Frank Lloyd Wright. However, his architecture is authentic, and each project an experiment leading to the next one while never ceasing to provide new elements, working with the materials to turn them into something beautiful. "As if it were an exercise in alchemy, the good architect and designer wishes to become one with excellence," according to one article in the Architectural Digest. Nevertheless, he claims to have learned from his father and architects of his generation: Kenzo Tange, Louis Kahn, Alvar Aalto and Renzo Piano.

Wright was a real trailblazer in the way he transformed modern architecture: Many of the discoveries of the European avant-garde had been made 20 years before

21. Tsirigakis House, Mykonos (Greece), 1997

Predio de Sa Fúa, Minorca (Spain), 1998

Predio de Sa Fúa, Minorca (Spain), 1998

Riera House, Sant Andreu de Llavaneres (Spain), 1986

22. Greenlandia, St. Petersburg (Russia), 2004

23. Riera House, Sant Andreu de Llavaneres (Spain), 1986

24. Monjo House, Minorca (Spain), 1990

25. Pamekas House, Mykonos (Greece), 2002

him. However, the principles, philosophy and thinking that drove his work are a long way away from that of the "isms" that shook up the world of art and architecture at the beginning of the 20th century. In fact, the fluid space (boundless, dynamic space as opposed to static, closed space), a key concept in modern architecture, was first investigated by Wright, who stood out from the other fathers of modern architecture on account of his opposition to extreme austerity. Wright, like Barba, reveals a remarkable degree of sensitivity towards the natural environment, and thus on a "significant" level with respect to physical matter and experience through the body. His basic principle: a view of the house nestling in its natural surroundings and opening out on to them through the use of terraces, overhanging roofs, and also including a new vision of the house interior. The fact that Wright's message had an influence on Europe is patently obvious in the factory for the Werkbund exhibition in Cologne in 1914, designed by Walter Gropius. Later, however, other interpretations would abandon the original message to foment the new spirit of Cubism. In the following image, Wright's influence on Barba is clear to see.
(Photo 22)

In Wright's article entitled "An Organic Architecture," it is possible to see connections between his philosophy and that of Javier Barba: "In organic architecture, it is absolutely impossible to regard the building as one thing, its accessories and equipment as another thing, and its location and environment as another. The spirit in which these buildings are conceived views all of this as a single item. It should all be meticulously planned in keeping with its own nature. [...] Transforming a human room in this way so that it becomes a perfect work of art [...] which can at the same time become a harmonious reality that meets such requirements in terms of color, shape and nature and truly expresses its character [...] with respect to various items including use, construction, space, materials, and decoration, with the ornament not being merely an added adornment but becoming a catalyst for the fundamental concept of the building. Usefulness is harnessed to pleasure." For him, "unity is the watchword." Barba's gaze, like that of Wright, is directed towards nature.

As far as unity is concerned, it is a concept that also links up with the Bauhaus. All the elements need to relate to the whole. Barba's designs include both the outdoor and indoor areas, thus resulting in furniture like sofas, for instance, in the living areas or functional shelves, which are designed as the continuation of the same architectural space, without any boundaries between the two. Hence, what is perceived is fluidity, as if all the components had agreed not to stand out, in order to create a harmonious whole.
(Photos 23, 24, 25)

CONCLUSION

The lesson to be learned is that it is better to work with nature and not against it. If Mies Van der Rohe understood architecture as being something that was alive and forever changing, in keeping with the will of an era translated into space, and that produced an architecture that did not look back at the past but was instead integrated in the present, bringing together customs and habitat or society and urban development, Barba does exactly the same – in harmony with his own time. He even adds the intelligence of feeling, in accordance with ethical principles linking people and the natural environment. Without playing down all the achievements of the modern movement and hence the Bauhaus: "what was once beautiful cannot be reproduced today just as it was, without us finding it wanting." However, there are architectural elements that recur over the centuries because they respond to deep human needs, and our road to happiness relies on them: in symmetry, for instance, or in the curved lines of certain objects. If Mies opted for formal simplicity, revealing the structures of his buildings and providing them with essential forms, Barba integrates architecture and nature with the intention of creating affinity, harmony and hence a feeling of wellbeing for the occupants. Because if we are what we eat, we are also what we inhabit. "Wherever lines and sketches are arranged adequately, that will be our ideal habitat" (Alain de Botton, *The Architecture of Happiness*).

Cristina Roselló Mozas

RIERA HOUSE

Sant Andreu de Llavaneres, Spain // 1986

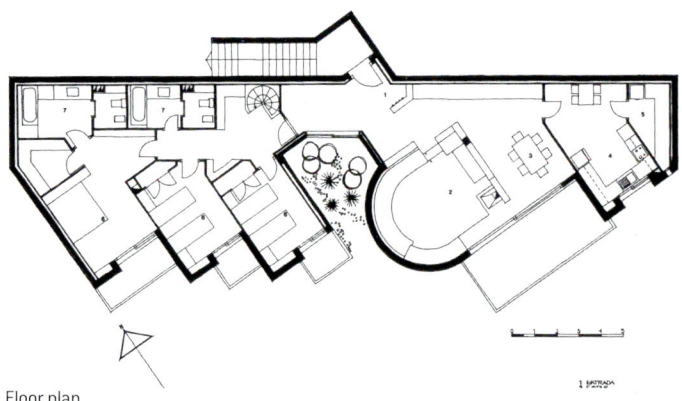

Floor plan

This family home is one of the first projects by Javier Barba and, indeed, the first bioclimatic project. The land had a steep slope in addition to a busy road crossing the top of the lot. These conditions, as well as the orientation and good views, led to the decision of half-burying the house. Thus, the roof is integrated into the natural slope of the mountain, minimizing the visual impact on the landscape and making use of natural thermal and acoustic insulation. The entry to the house resembles the entrance to a cave: a few steps lead into the hall, which opens onto a courtyard through which the light floods into the main living room. The elongated floor plan faces south, so that all rooms and spaces enjoy natural light. In addition, the position on the land encourages the circulation of air, one of the most basic passive elements of sustainable architecture. All rooms, in turn, offer spectacular views of the Mediterranean coast.

Partially burying the house and installing green roofs achieves significant energy savings all year round. Striated thick concrete walls, a material that provides thermal inertia are a noteworthy feature. The predominance of straight lines in the plan of the house is only broken by the semicircular design of one of the walls which houses the living room, whose sofa follows its curve.

This project was selected by the European Commission within the Project Monitor Program in 1989, and in the George Wright Forum, as an example of one of the world's best sustainable houses, integrated into the environment.

16 // SINGLE FAMILY DETACHED HOME

MONJO HOUSE

Minorca, Spain // 1990

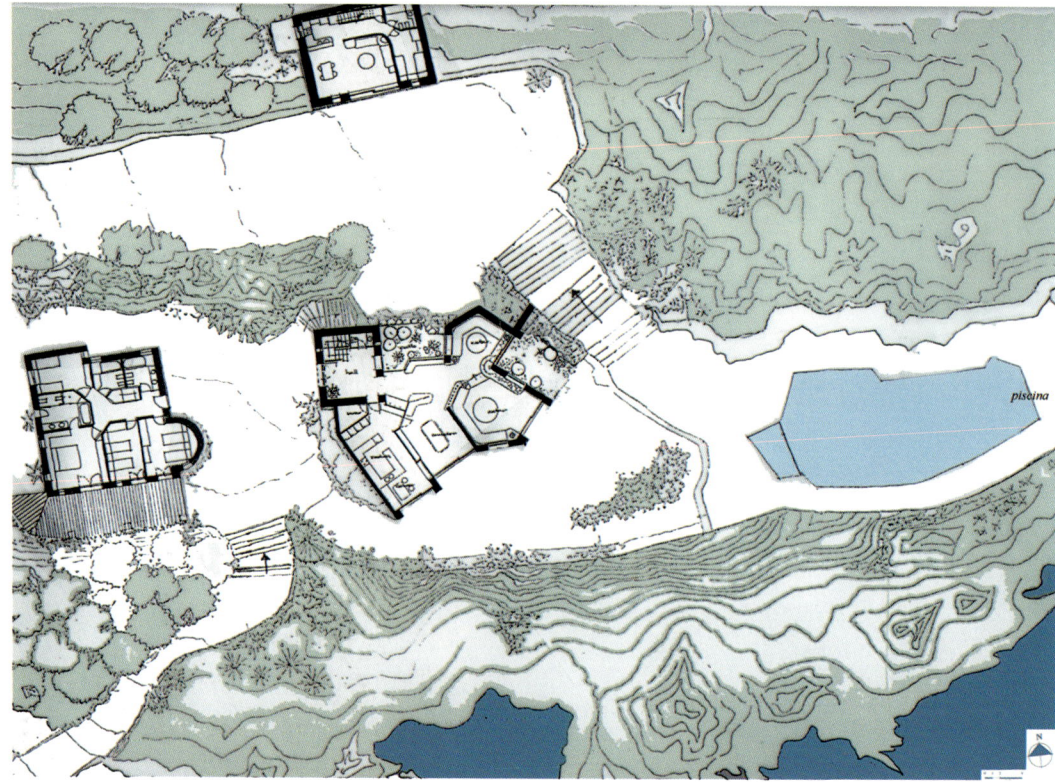

General plan

The main challenge of this project was to construct on a predominant point in Cala Pregonda, in the north of Minorca, without modifying the charm and beauty of the landscape.

In order to study the terrain and find inspiration to design this summer house, Javier Barba and his family camped on the site for a week. During that time, Barba came to the conclusion that the main inspirational features should be the existing landscape and the sea.

To integrate the house into this natural environment, he used the stone from the excavation, thus unifying the volumes that make up the façade. In this way the building seems to emerge from the rock. Looking from the sea, it is difficult to distinguish the house from the cliff, as its irregular form and texture of rock is brilliantly integrated into the landscape.

The structure of this project is comprised of three volumes. In the central unit, which houses the common areas, the main feature is an old stone tower, which was incorporated into the project as an entrance area and that has guest rooms in the upper storey. The other bedrooms are in the annex building, and there is an apartment for guests in the highest level. These three modules are connected internally and externally through terraces, corridors and stone staircases. The roof, bordered with vegetation, becomes another terrace in the garden. The *Architectural Digest* magazine chose this project for its January 1992 cover, dedicated to Spain for the Olympic Games.

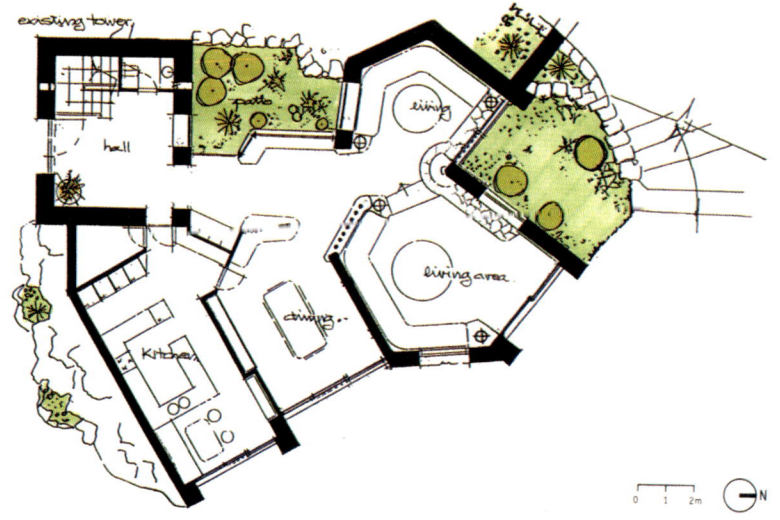

Ground floor plan of the main residence

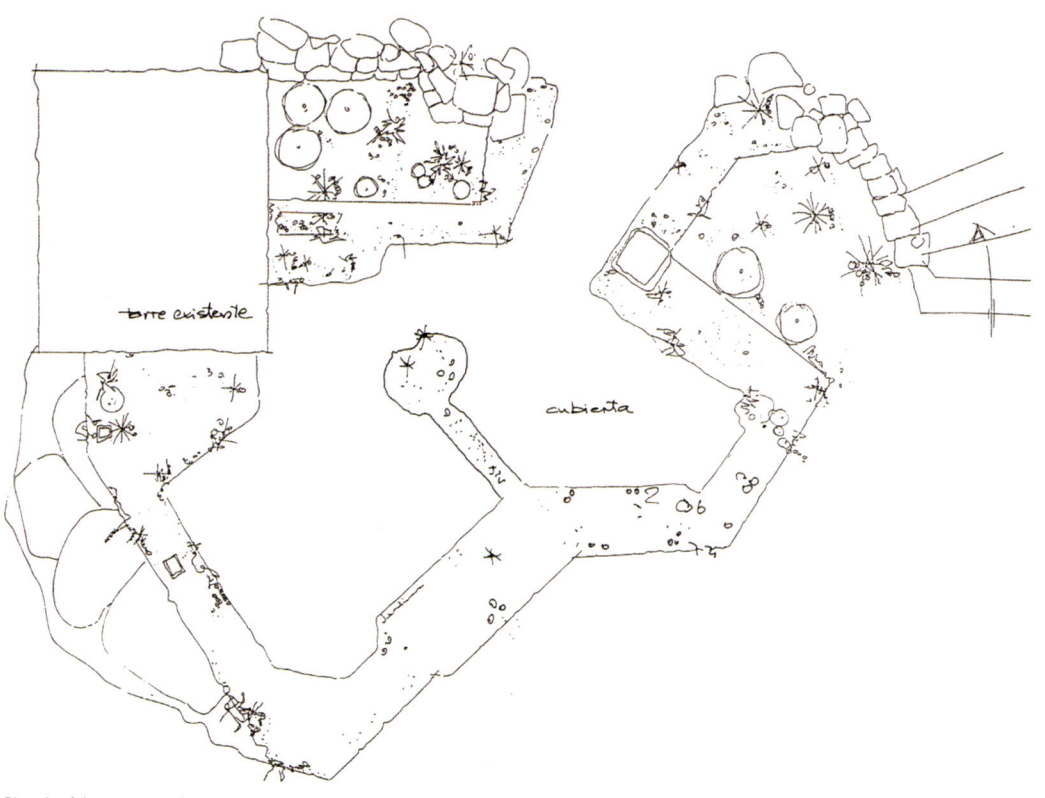

Sketch of the green roof

Guest house

MONJO HOUSE // 25

CARALPS HOUSE

Alella, Spain // 1989

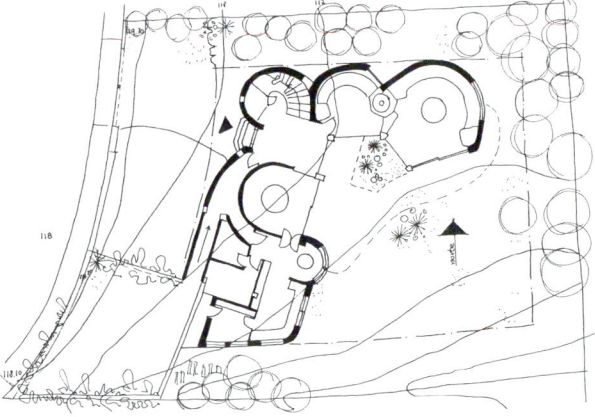

Ground floor plan

Pure, straight lines interchange with the curved forms across the façade of this dwelling facing the Mediterranean, in a village near Barcelona. The chipped concrete is the main element of the exterior finish, combined with metal frames; it gives the building a sober air. This two-storey dwelling is built on a 10,763 sq ft lot. The first floor is destined for daytime use while the upper floor is for night time use.

To the right of the entrance to the lot there is a ramp leading to the garage; its buried roof is integrated into the garden.

The first floor consists of two areas: to the right of the entrance is the kitchen, servant's room with bath and dining room, and to the left, there are two living rooms linked by a fireplace, and a circular staircase leading to the second floor where the bedrooms are located. The idea of planning two different living rooms responds to the owners' desire to create a more intimate and warm space around the fire in winter, and another more spacious area in touch with the garden and pool for the rest of the year.

The project was completed with a tranquil garden surrounding the house. All the plants used, which at different points break up the imposing concrete façade, are of Mediterranean origin. In short, this is a house with a functional design that allows the residents to live surrounded by nature.

CARALPS HOUSE // 27

SEMEL HOUSE

Sant Andreu de Llavaneres, Spain // 1985

This family home is one of the first projects developed by Javier Barba. It is part of a development of five houses built in Llavaneres, in narrow and deep lots located in a pine forest near the sea.

The project design responds to the desire to protect the house from the wind, overcome the slope of the land and attain the best sea views.

A staircase made of wooden sleepers in the middle of a rock garden leads to the main entrance of the house, crossing the garden skirting the long, irregular pool which includes a waterfall.

The house, situated to the rear of the lot to make better use of the garden, has two floors plus a basement. The first floor houses the living room, dining room and kitchen, while the bedrooms are upstairs. The basement is used as a games and service room and leads out to a back courtyard.

One of the most noteworthy elements of the project is the curved eaves that form the porch and becomes the green roof of the upper part. When you open the windows of the bedrooms the roof appears to be a vast garden, with the pinetree-covered hills as a backdrop.

The use of black slate slabs creates a stark contrast to the white plastered walls. This combination of materials is inspired by the house in Cadaqués where the architect used to spend his summers, a house designed by his father and which featured the same materials.

The purchase of the apartment by a German family, who are friends of the family, completed the construction project of this first development carried out with his partner and friend Javier Pérez del Pulgar.

MORA HOUSE

Calella de Palafrugell, Spain // 1989

This project's client was a friend of Javier Barba, therefore, with total confidence he suggested that the architect did what he believed most appropriate. The site is located on the Costa Brava, a privileged spot in the hills near the town of Calella and a few minutes from the seashore. A farmhouse stood in the middle of this lot, of which part of the volume and the irregular stone on the façades was preserved, thus maintaining its essence. The result were two separate volumes: one, the old volume, transformed into a two-story building containing the bedrooms, clad in stone, the other, a newly constructed volume in colored concrete. These are connected by the entrance area, which acts as a junction between the two modules.

Stone is also used in the common areas, both inside and outside, but in a more refined texture. The hexagonal shaped living room invites gatherings. Irregular slate stones were used for the flooring. The circular green roof designed over the common areas considerably overhangs the perimeter of these rooms, creating a spacious porch. Initially a cantilevered roof was planned, but finally the architect decided to support it on columns that allow for the draining of the green roof. The landscape design was done by the landscape designer Ana Esteve.

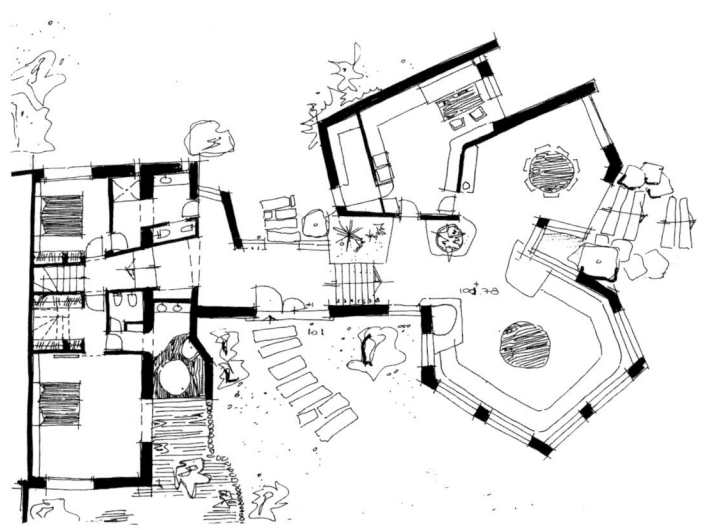
Floor plan

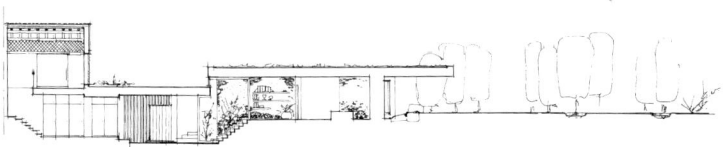
Longitudinal section

Façade

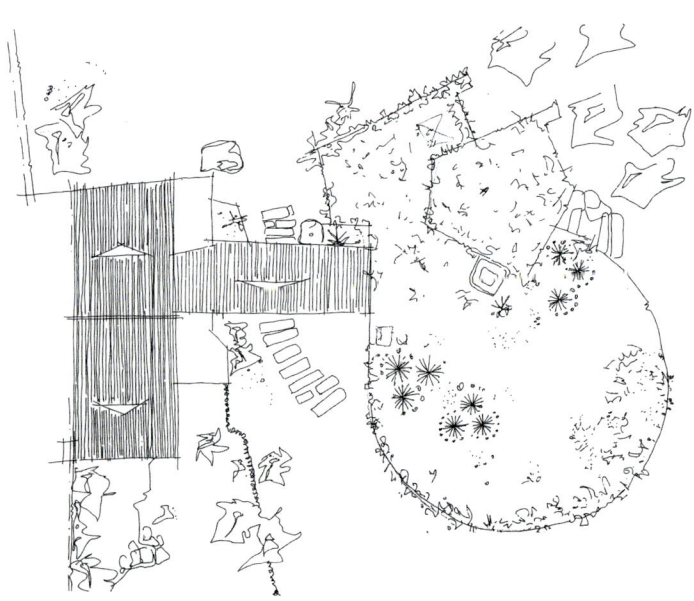

Roof plan

32 // SINGLE FAMILY DETACHED HOME

GIRÓ SUMMER PAVILION

Sitges, Spain // 1995

Located a few kilometers from Barcelona, Sitges is one of the few towns on the Catalan coast that has retained its essence and, in a sense, it escapes, the aggressive overcrowding typical of coastal towns. In its residential area, facing the sea and next to the promenade, the Noucentisme and contemporary houses stand out.

A married couple, friends of Javier Barba and owners of a neoclassical villa in this neighborhood, asked for his help to design a swimming pool. The architect proposed to complement the pool with an adjoining area: a space that included a living room/dining room, a kitchen-bar and a bathroom-dressing room. This was conceived as an informal extension of the house that would be used in particular during the summer months. The rectangular structure with perimetral eaves has one opaque side and the other transparent. The windowless, wood-clad side contains the dressing rooms. The living room/dining room opens onto the pool through large glass French doors.

A little paved pathway borders the building, leading to a solarium around the pool. A green roof was also designed both for its insulating and aesthetic properties. As a result, this pavilion, seen from the top floor of the main volume of the house, looks like a carpet of flowers. Inside warm ocher tones in different textures, travertine flooring, plaster on the walls and built-in furniture were used. At the request of the owner, the ensemble is complemented with a combination of fresco-style accessories such as furniture and one of the walls. The owner also found a unique piece that stands out among the furniture: a dining table that turns into a standard pool table.

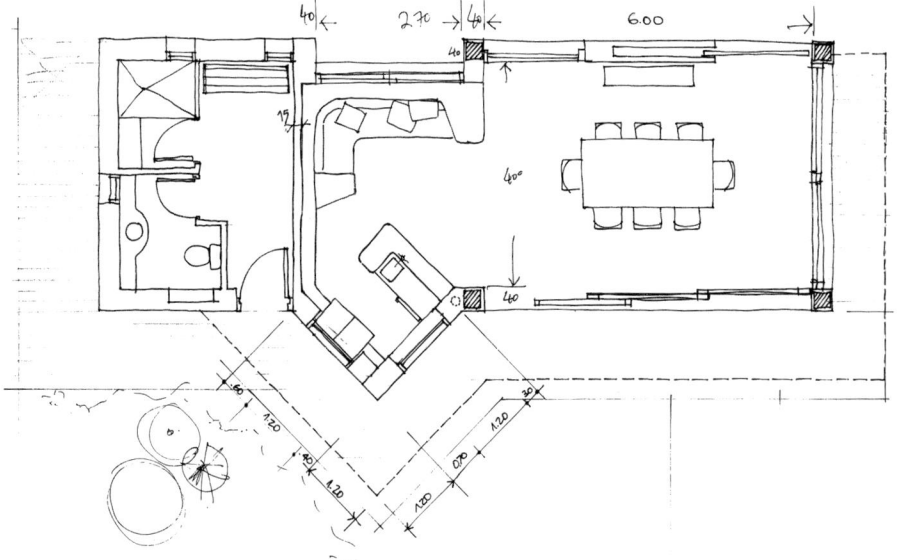

General plan

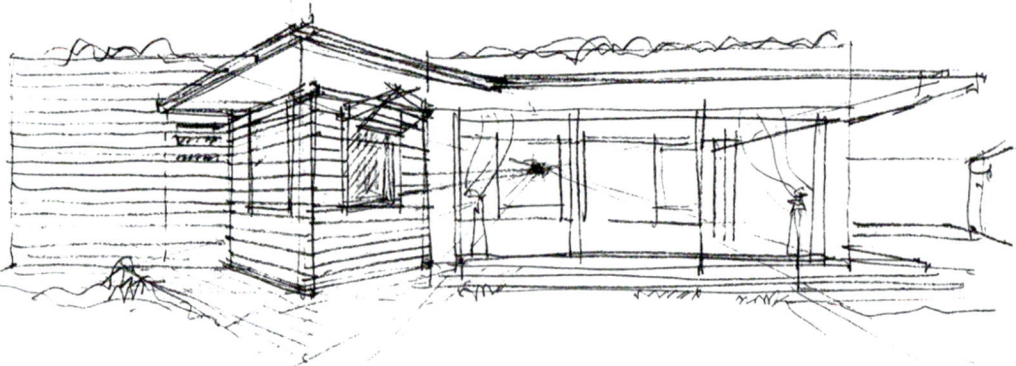

Perspective

36 // SINGLE FAMILY DETACHED HOME

MORA HOUSE

Llafranc, Spain // 1997

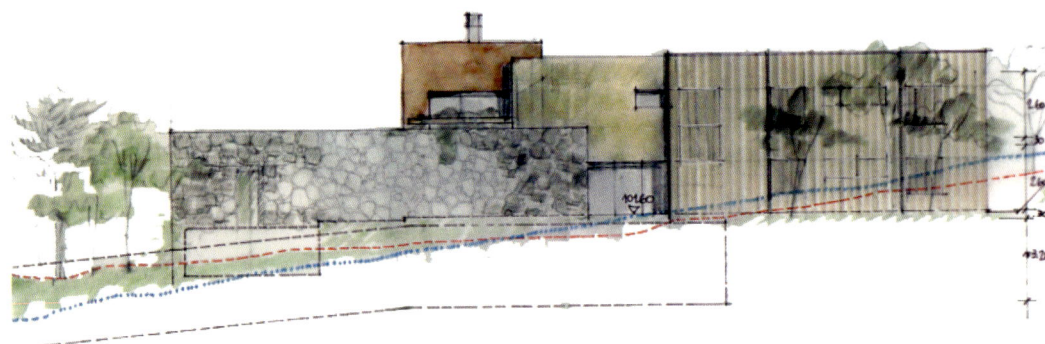

East elevation

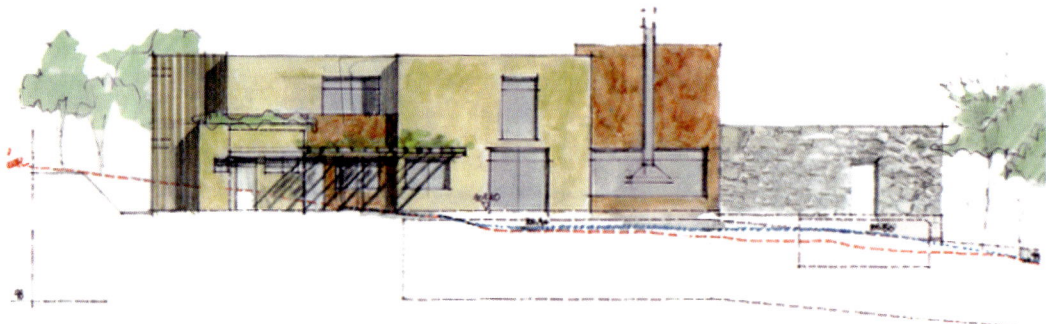

West elevation

A close friend of Javier Barba asked the architect to build a summer house for his family in Llafranc, a coastal town in Catalonia. This construction had to be developed on a site in the heart of town.

The complicated location of the site, excellent for its proximity to the sea, but on a corner of a busy street set the ground rules for the project proposal. The architect decided to close off the most exposed side of the lot with a wall, acting as a screen to protect the house from the noise. This screen is integrated into the environment and it has a variety of different finishes: at the start, it is a rusty llicorella stone wall (locally sourced), which then changes to a basic plaster volume that frames the entrance and ends with a wall clad in wood.

As the plan was designed for a large family, the size of the lot and planning regulations allowed for a two storey house plus basement, which is distributed over several volumes on two different levels. The first floor overlooking the bay of Llafranc, including common areas and service areas, is open to the south with a courtyard and a pool. The bedrooms on the upper level have access to the terraces and the green roof. In the basement, the large garage includes space for cars and for a small boat. The inspiration for the two-toned ocher façade was taken from the colors of the stone used, which along with the paneled wall, create a harmony of colors in the finishes. The limited color palette and pure lines of the walls give the house a pleasant feeling of solidity.

Perspective

ZERMOMA HOUSE

Ibiza, Spain // 2000

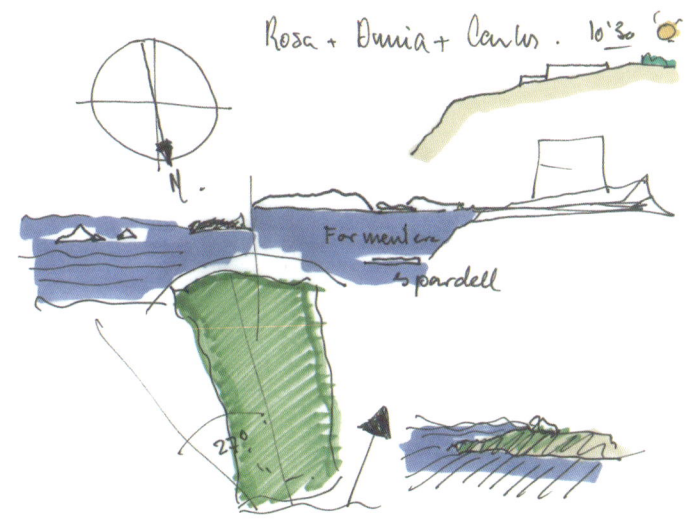

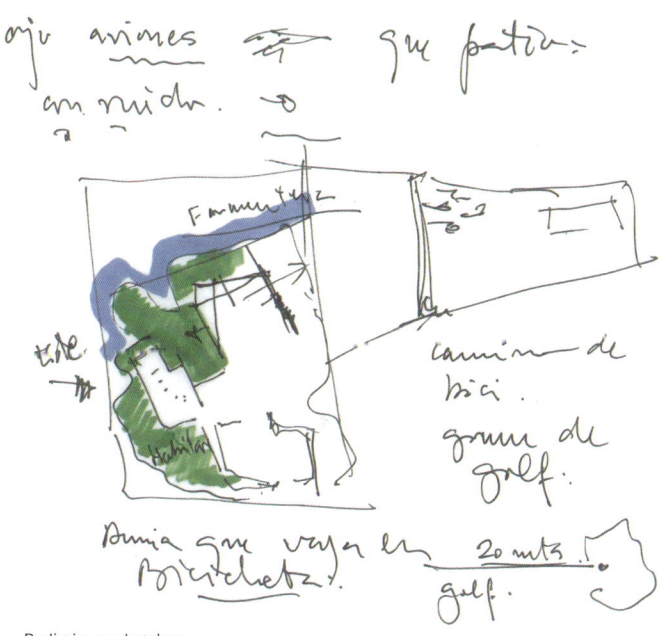

Preliminary sketches

The entrance courtyard was designed as a starting point of the project, around which the different areas of the house are organized. The priority was to take full advantage of the panoramic views that this location enjoys: to the left you can see Santa Eulalia, opposite, Formentera, and to the right, Dalt Vila, the historic old town of Ibiza. Good orientation to the south and from east to west, the topography of the site, which descends to the sea and the determining urban factors, also influenced the layout of this house.

A pleasant trail winds along one hundred meters, connecting the public road to the courtyard entrance of the house. The living area is basically on the first floor. The upper floor has a study with access to the outdoors and the lower levels can be reached through the garden, where there is a swimming pool and solarium, as well as two guest apartments.

The hall, overlooking the sea, separates the communal and private areas. The constructed volume is interspersed with other smaller courtyards between the different rooms to integrate the entire plan into the setting. All courtyards are linked to the outer edges of the porches fitted with pergolas.

Apart from the main body of the house, there is a large terrace built at a 180º angle. The stone walls that punctually stand out from the façade are responsible for defining the different outdoor areas The slope of the land has been maintained through a rock garden and vegetation, bordering the staircase that connects the garden on the first floor with the pool.

General plan

Housing and pool area

ZERMOMA HOUSE // 47

BARBA HOUSE ESTATE KALANDRIA

Delta de l'Ebre, Spain // 2000

This twenty hectare family farm with 2,500 olive trees is located on a high valley overlooking the Ebro delta and the sea. The site is shaped like a peninsula, as it is limited by two canyons. Two houses were built on the site, one main house and one for guests, separated by 1,312 ft, which maintains privacy. Halfway along the path there is a stone building used for storing solar cells and as a studio.

Two curved stone walls enclose the ample space on the first floor of the main dwelling, which contains the common areas, a bedroom, a bathroom and storage space. The suite overlooking the delta is on the top floor. Outside an outdoor eating area with barbecue was designed.

Due to its location on the site and the position of the windows, the sun enters the house according to the seasons, regulating the comfort of the rooms. The first floor is warm in winter, due to the temperature and atmosphere created by the sunlight, and fresh and airy in summer, thereby fulfilling one of the basic principles of bioclimatic architecture.

The ensemble was designed to be self-sufficient and solar energy is harnessed through photovoltaic cells to generate electricity and solar panels for hot water. The project is inspired by the vernacular house with pitched roofs to collect rainwater. Materials that stand out include tiles, the use of local stone, plaster in ocher shades, terracotta tiles and woodwork.

This site, a biosphere reserve an hour and a half from Barcelona, close to the sea, overlooking the Ebro delta and surrounded by agricultural areas is tranquil, private and quiet, meeting the conditions that the architect and his family demanded.

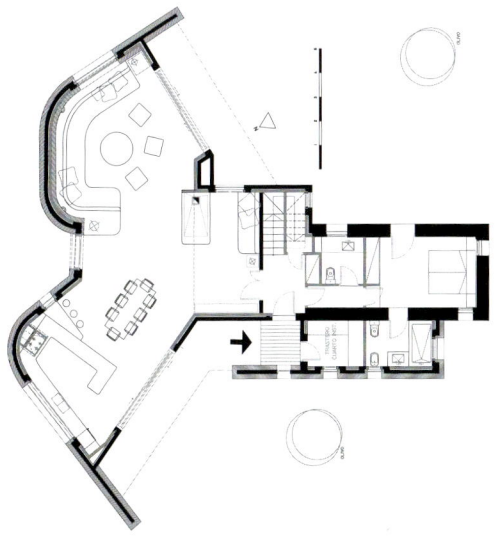
Ground floor plan

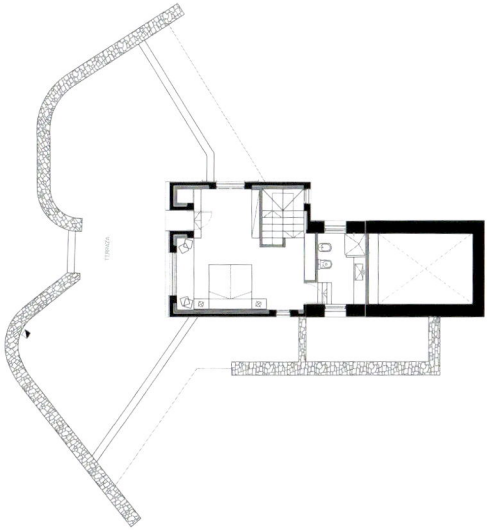
Upper floor plan

On these pages:
guesthouse

PI SUNYER HOUSE

Cadaqués, Spain // 1999

The color combination created by the slate stone, the main material used in the project, gives character to this home. The sober gray tones is broken by the shades of brown, red and orange to bring warmth to the volume, whose pitched roofs form a set of slopes. This family house is on a rectangular site. The wider side has unobstructed panoramic views over the bay of Cadaqués. The houses linear approach establishes two entrances: one for vehicles at street level and a pedestrian entrance at a higher level. The higher level was designed as a large landscaped area, bordered by a stone wall and a part of the façade of the house. The entrance, located in the center of the first floor, divides the different areas: to the northwest are the bedrooms, whose axis coincides with the living area and to the southeast the kitchen, laundry room and dining room.

The linear plan is interrupted by a patio, partly covered with a pergola, including the common area, the porch and a guest room. As an extension of this porch, there is an infinity pool. The distribution of the areas allows the exterior spaces to be differentiated in terms of both size and uses, separated by way of private terraces at different levels in the sleeping area and creating a large courtyard for outdoor activities. On the lower level there is a basement that is used as a garage. Inside, the house may be perceived as both sober and warm, some of the furniture is built-in, for example in the kitchen, bathroom and the library. Plants are a constant element in this project and are incorporated into the house around the boundary of the house.

Sea elevation

Mountain elevation

PI SUNYER HOUSE // 59

IRBESAMA HOUSE

Baix Empordà, Spain // 2007

A lot in the housing development of Empordà Golf Club is the location for the second residence of a South African couple with three children. Reconciling the needs of the family and the topography and building code led to the layout of the plan that crosses the land from east to west and organizes the house in order to procur the best orientation and views. The interesting location adds value to the project, as to the north it is bordered by one of the lakes of the golf course and to the east, its interior roads.

The same volume arranges and divides the various outdoor spaces. Inside, the living room-dining room and the porch are located in the central part of the first floor to spatially and visually capture the beauty of the place and link the two areas of the garden. On one side, to the southeast, the garden with pool is designed as an extension of the porch, while the other side of the garden, next to the lake, boasts a decked area as an extension of the house and the guest rooms. The latter can be accessed from the same room or via the porch.

Pedestrian access and the garage door of this two storey house are located to the front of this site. The first floor includes the aforementioned common and service areas, as well as an area for children with a game room. The top floor can be accessed via the stairs, located in the hall. To one side is the master bedroom suite, with a dressing room and terrace, and towards the front, the other bedrooms with their own bathrooms and terraces.

The façade has been treated by combining three materials in line with Estudio BC's design principles: wood, natural stone and plastered surfaces, in earth colors influenced by the local color range.

TUSQUETS HOUSE

Barcelona, Spain // 2009

This family home is located in the upper area of Barcelona. The project proposed to move the building to the rear of the site in order to achieve the best orientation towards the south and east, and to have a spacious garden. Furthermore, building the house on the highest point of the land attains the best views of the sea, the city of Barcelona and also the Serra de Collserola. Its proximity to a ring road required a formal solution to noise pollution. Estudio BC resolved this in the home, by designing a wooden skin formed by vertical slats, which covers the back and side façade, and planning a green wall-slope on the edge of the lot that reinforces the protection against the noise.

The pedestrian access to the house through the garage is located to the side of the site from the lowest level. The main entrance is located in the middle part of the first floor. The different floors, first, second, third and basement are designed following the longitudinal form of the terrain, with a stairwell and elevator in the middle that divides the different areas in each level. The basement as well as the garage includes storage rooms, exercise room, wine cellar and a gym at the back of the garden. The hall divides the space on the first floor: to the left are the living areas, opposite this the dining room and to the right the kitchen office and service areas. The bedrooms, along with a studio and terraces, are on the second floor while the master bedroom is on the third floor, which is also equipped with terraces.

The contrast between the wood and bush-hammered concrete with large woodwork structures serves to integrate the house with the garden and its surroundings. The project includes a lap pool.

TUSQUETS HOUSE // 67

LORD ROTHSCHILD SUMMER PAVILION

Corfu, Greece // 1993

Before Javier Barba received this commision, the owner had previously ruled out interesting proposals from renowned international architects. The main objective was to integrate the construction into this beautiful spot on the island of Corfu. None of the projects submitted had managed to find a balance between the footprint of the construction and this virgin enclave. Collaboration with the studio came about by chance when the owner saw a project by Javier Barba on the cover of the U.S. magazine *Architectural Digest* in the issue dedicated to Spain for the Olympics, and he was amazed at the skill with which Barba had integrated the construction into the natural environment. So he contacted him. When Javier studied the land, he made a great discovery: an ancient marble quarry was buried in a steep promontory of the land, and a vein of marble became the main feature of the project.

This pavilion is characterized by the element of surprise, because from above it is hidden and the different areas are gradually discovered. First of all the access to the pavilion is located at the rear. A courtyard with a fountain are the main features of the entrance and, beyond the arches, there is the service area and a Roman bath. Finally, there is a porch and a pool. A Roman mosaic on the floor of the porch is integrated into the travertine floor. Local stone, tiles and marble harmonize the pavilion with the land, while water falls down the irregular rock that flanks the pool area. The massive pool is filled with sea water. The project was planned as a reinterpretation of the traditional architecture of the Ionian island, with a clear Italian influence.

STRONGILLO
RESIDE
KANONAS.

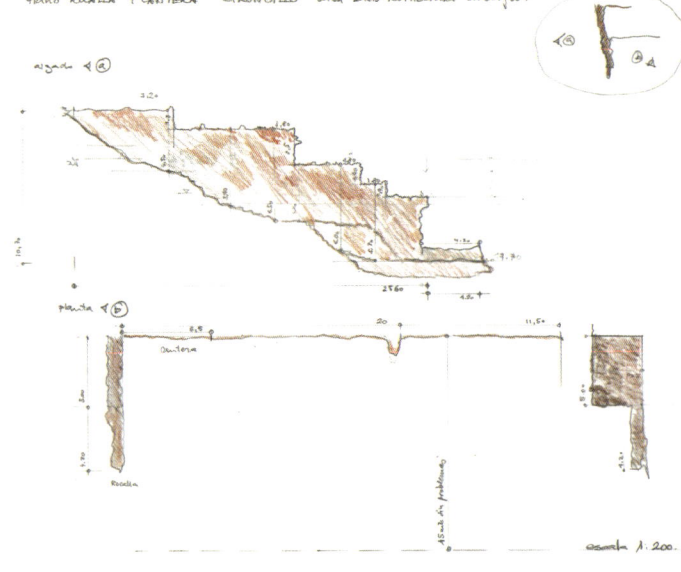

Plano ROCALLA Y CANTERA STRONGILLO casa Lord Rothschild en Corfú.

escala 1:200.

74 // SINGLE FAMILY DETACHED HOME

Sea elevation

Perspectives

TSIRIGAKIS HOUSE

Mykonos, Greece // 1997

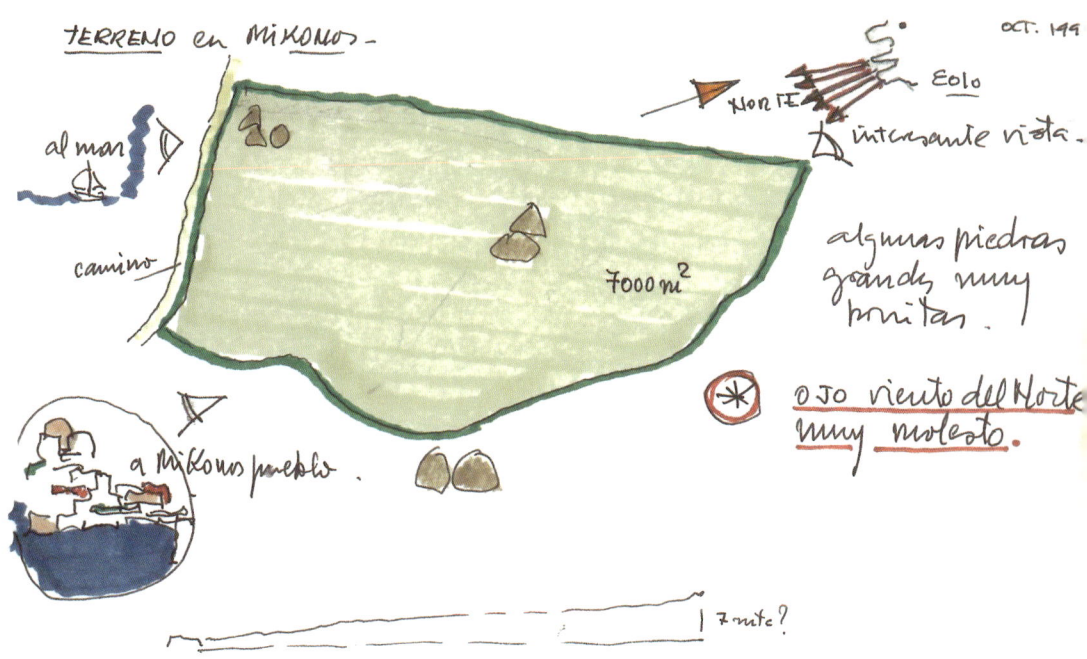

Field survey

An existing large rock located in the central and highest point of the land, from which you can see the whole area, including the town of Mykonos and the port, is the absolute protagonist of this project. Given its size and strategic position, it was the origin of this project, integrating it into the land. To the left are the common areas — the living room, dining room, kitchen and service quarters — and to the right, the master suite and the rest of the bedrooms.

In order to protect the home from the strong north wind, called Meltemi, which batters this area of the Aegean Sea in summer, large stone walls were designed creating the different spaces. These walls offer privacy to the rooms and protect the pool area and the traditional porch, overlooking the port. They also create a sheltered courtyard which is the access to the main entrance of the house.

To integrate the work into the environment and respect the traditional vernacular of the island, the house was built with stone and other local materials. The traditional white stucco, common to the Greek islands, covers the rounded profiles, which contrast with the straight walls. These winding forms result in a dome-shaped structure over the bathtub of the main suite, creating a unique space. Several white chimneys that resemble lookouts crown the roof of the house. Natural light bathes all the interior rooms, designed in light and airy colors. An impressive rock stands out among the arches and columns, traditional wooden beams and beech wood flooring. It is the undisputed main feature of the project, and it brings the residents into close contact with nature.

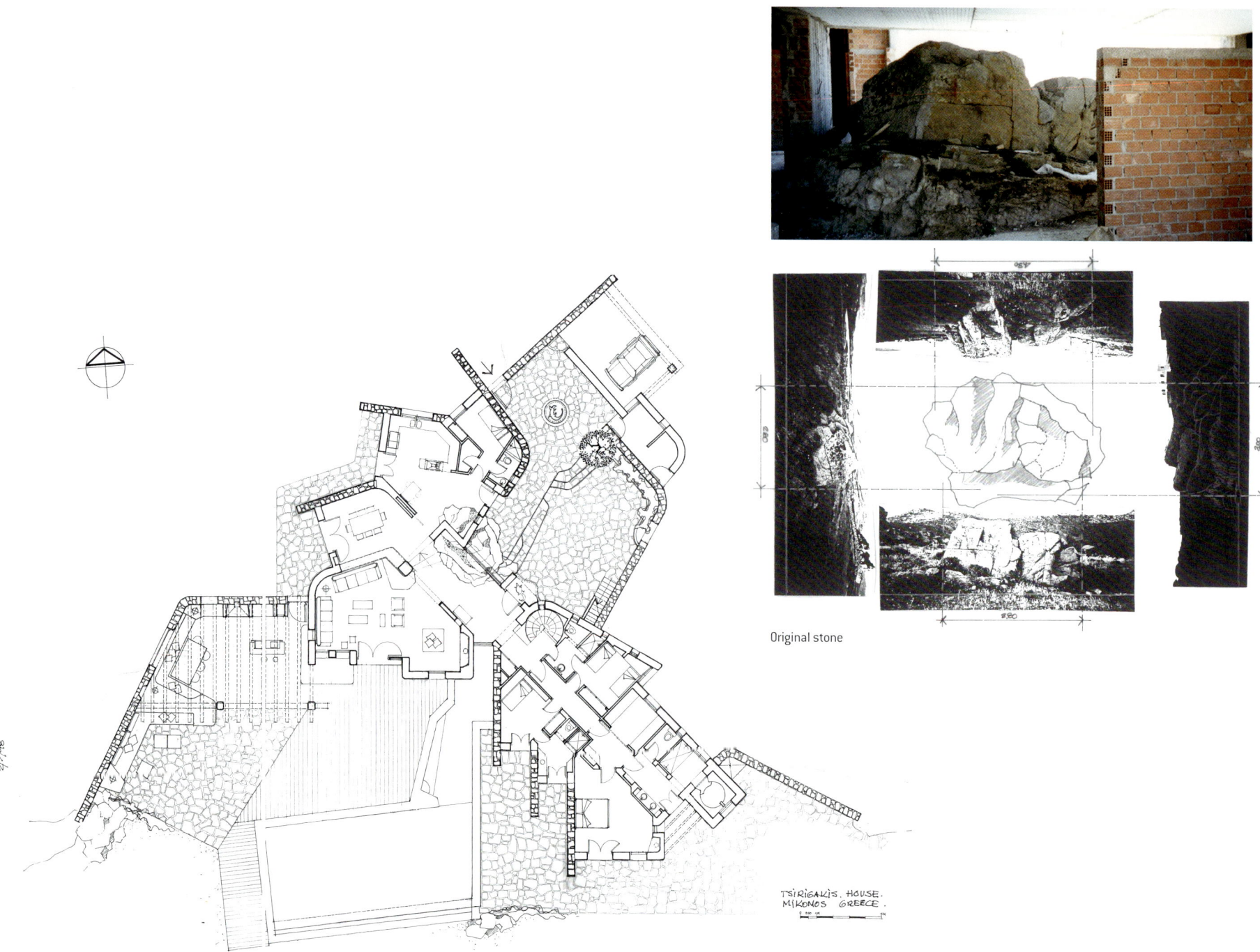

Original stone

TSIRIGAKIS HOUSE.
MIKONOS GREECE.

DELIGIANNIS HOUSE

Mykonos, Greece // 2000

This house is located on a large lot near the beach of Lia, southeast of the island of Mykonos. A priority was given to solving the problems created by the island's natural conditions, such as its rugged terrain and the four strong winds that batter it, when designing the house. So, the project has a double courtyard differentiated by its use. The widest contains the garage area with a pergola, while the other, with planted trees and located directly opposite the main entrance, is protected by high stone walls that form its perimeter.

The creation of emotion is one of the objectives of the project, and this is achieved perfectly when you cross the threshold, where a large window in the hall surprises the visitor with a series of wonderful views – first of all, the pond, then the infinity pool and finally the sea. The same hall separates the two living areas, which were designed on a single level with a linear structure. To one side the bedrooms, bathrooms and master suite are laid out, positioned at the back to offer privacy. The other area contains the common areas, accessed via a few steps leading to a porch, a bar and a barbecue area. The thick walls, irregular-shaped cubes, the different heights and the rough texture evoke and respect the traditional style of houses in Mykonos.

A priority was given to solving the problems created by the island's natural conditions, such as its rugged terrain and the four strong winds that batter it, when designing the house.

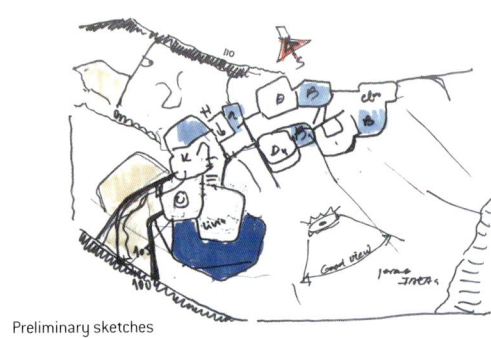

Preliminary sketches

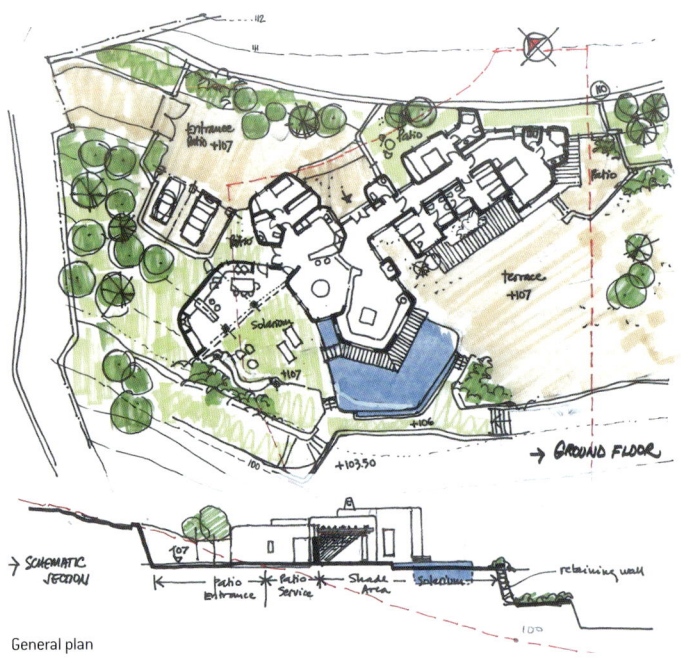

General plan

Elevations

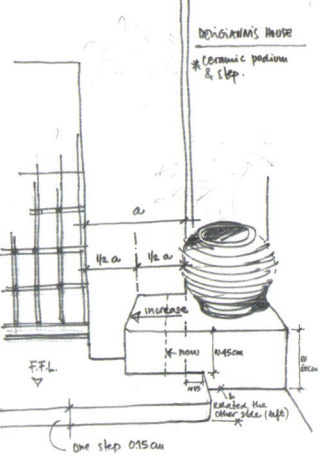

KOKKALIS HOUSE

Mykonos, Greece // 2001

Field survey

From the outset, the force of the elements that come together in this enclave determined the project. Its unique geography, earth colors, rocks, the deep blue sea and the bright white architecture helped to achieve one of Estudio BC's basic premises: respect for the environment and the integration of the project into the landscape.

The program included a summer residence consisting of two buildings, located on a rocky promontory overlooking the town of Mykonos and its port, and from where you can view the outline of other Aegean islands. The units were designed around a tower similar to an ancient fortress and are connected by stone walls. These walls organize the outdoor spaces and create shaded areas, cliff edge walks and the entrance along the pathway. The two houses face the sun and the views, and are protected from northerly winds.

In order to improve integration and privacy, the rock in the site was cut to adapt to the foundations of the house, for this reason different heights can be perceived. From the entrance road, the volume appears to have one level but from the sea, you can appreciate the different levels forming terraces. The common areas and the main suite are on the first floor, the guest rooms overlooking the pool and the bay of Mykonos are on the lower level. The interior design was carried out along with the owner, who opted for a mixture of antique and contemporary pieces. The courtyards feature ancient Greek pots and a huge old oak and iron portals from the Xian dynasty. This project was published in the August 2007 issue of the *Architectural Digest*.

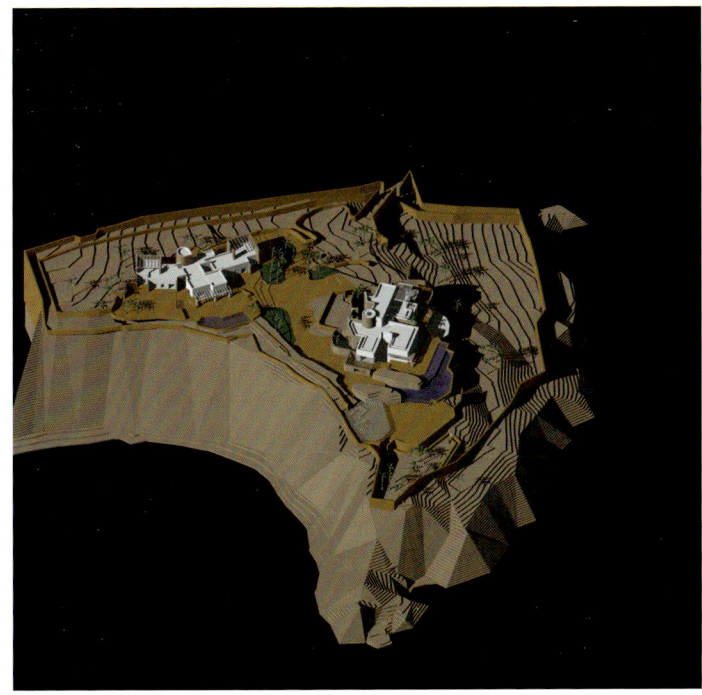

KOKKALIS HOUSE // 103

PAMEKAS HOUSE

Mykonos, Greece // 2002

The beauty of the location, protected by the geography of this part of the coast, provides the ideal framework for the design of this home, in which the owners enthusiastically participated during the construction work.

The house is arranged on two levels, both with direct access due to the slope of the land: an upper-level housing the bedrooms accessed through a patio and an adjacent parking lot and the main level on the first floor, which is in contact with the land. A landscaped ramp on either side leads to the large wooden doorway, framed by bamboo, bougainvillea and an old olive tree. From this point, there is a large esplanade that leads to the home. On the left there is a shaded parking lot and in front you can see the high, white volumes of the houses, with two smooth curved stone walls that frame the entrance.

On the first floor, which houses the common areas, neutral colors that unify the space and provide warmth prevail.

Simplicity permeates all areas of this home. Open spaces that seek functionality in an austere and elegant way are a feature that is repeated on the outside with a large stone paved terraced area where the house and the large porch are located. Together they form a large minimalist platform which complements the surrounding landscape, making it stand out. The large porch is supported by a retaining wall made from local stone. At the edge of the site, beyond the porch, there is an area for guests. The infinity pool and the skilled gardening work, with herbs, shrubs and trees, complete the space of this simple and welcoming home.

PAMEKAS HOUSE // 109

ECONOMOU – VOSNIADES HOUSES

Skiathos, Greece // 2008

The island of Skiathos, part of the Sporades archipelago, has interesting landscape and architectural features, which combine the blue sea, the lush hills with pines and olive trees, and white-walled, tiled-roof buildings.

The site on which the house was built, almost 328 ft long, literally descends to the sea with a slope of 30%. Access is from the upper part, at an elevation of 105 ft, and the complex reaches the sea level.

The program included a main house with a separate apartment on the top floor for the daughter and two small separate houses for the two adult children. Each unit has two floors. Although all three buildings belong to the same family, this approach allows the family to have independence and privacy. The complex also boasts a sports area, a tennis court and a porch with barbecue area, swimming pool and solarium.

Based on the conditions of the terrain and the program, the key to the project was the design of connections from a side street that serves as an access to each house, an arduous job to create functional exterior spaces in perfect relation to the houses and guaranteed sea views. The slopes and retaining walls create parking spaces, pergolas and terraces. There is also a pedestrian walkway with steps that connect the complex.

Using local architecture as an exemplar, through the inclination of the walls and roofs the white volumes are reinforced. The result of the fusion of these buildings in a terrain with steep slopes, varied volumes, pedestrian paths and access for vehicles, terraces and a solarium coverts this project into a small private resort, exclusive for the family.

TERZOPOULOS HOUSE

Athens, Greece // 2001

This house is situated in a residential area near Athens, overlooking the surrounding hills. The lot has a slope in the opposite direction to the access road. To maximize the use of the land and for better orientation, an L-shape plan was chosen, with the rest of the space used for the garden and outdoor living areas. The volume is organized into three floors: the basement, the first floor which houses the common areas and, finally, the top floor where the bedrooms are located.

The sobriety that the pure lines of the cubic volumes of the house transmit, with plastered surfaces painted in warm colors, contrasts with the texture of the stone walls.

The windows and balconies have been designed to take advantage of the sun during the winter and provide shelter from it during warmer months. This passive solar energy is one of the most common solutions that bioclimatic architecture incorporates. Each of the openings frames a different area of the garden, which can be seen from the interior as natural, changing squares.

Special interest was put into the design of the access, located in the corner of the building. This open space is conceived as a small glass box with wooden panels. This area, composed of the hall and staircase is the interface between the two wings of the house.

Several types of vegetation are combined in the garden, from lawn, and climbing plants to small bushes and several varieties of trees. The solarium and swimming pool are located at a lower level at the bottom of the lot.

Façades study

RALLIS HOUSE

Athens, Greece // 2003

The corner site is located in a residential area north of Athens. The house occupies half of the site, assigning more area to the garden with views of Mount Penteli. The client, who was very participative during the project, from the outset proposed a very detailed program for this family with three children and two dogs. The house has two levels: the first floor contains the common areas and four bedrooms, and the lower level houses the studio, multimedia room, gym, guest bedrooms, service areas and garage. This level has sections which open out onto the garden creating the façade given the unevenness of the terrain. On the roof, the client requested a lounge area to view the sky.

Curved lines are the feature of this project. The project defines a gentle but forceful way of relating to the exterior space, and makes the interior spaces unique. The entrance is flanked by two curved walls, one of which is a cylindrical volume containing the staircase. From the hall, the two wings of the house can be seen, separated by a narrow, deep courtyard: to the left are the various common areas, perfectly defined but which are perceived as a single large space, to the right, the bedrooms, where the curved stone walls of the suite stand out and which form the fireplace.

Local stone, timber and wood paneling are features both inside and outside, creating continuity and harmony. The careful landscaping can be appreciated in the garden. The existing pine trees were maintained as a hallmark on the site, giving elegance to the lot, combined with old olive trees, vines and herbs. A long, narrow pool completes this space.

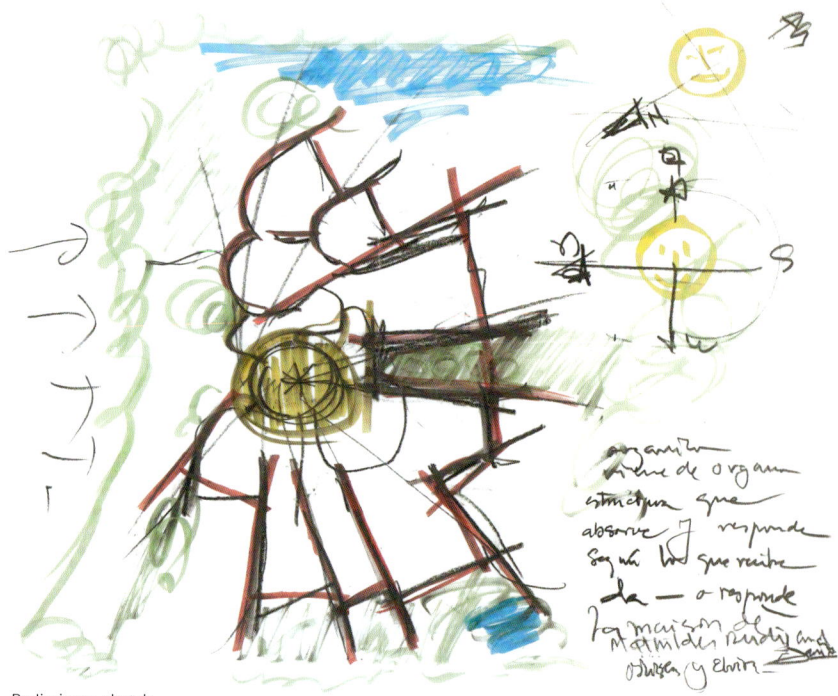

Preliminary sketch

House access

Ground floor plan

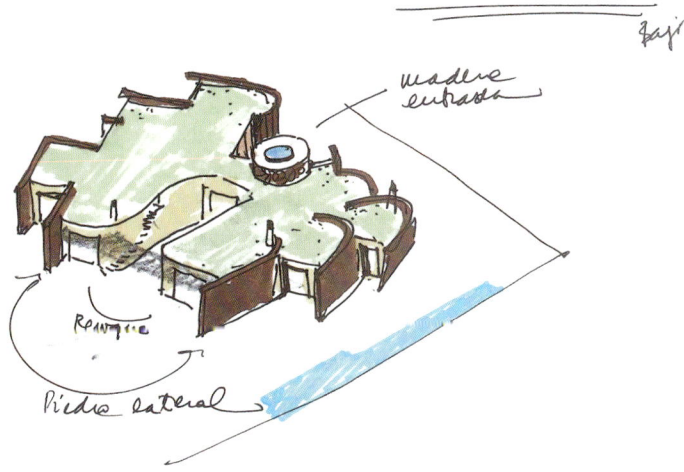

Axonometric view

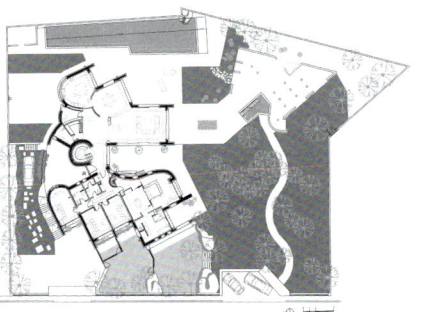
General plan

Bedroom and access from outside

PARASCHIS HOUSE

Koilada, Greece // 2009

View of the site

Sketches of the general plan

Due to the topography, and in order to maximize the views and the best orientation, this family house located two hours from Athens was distributed to provide proper sunlight through the use of courtyards and roof lighting. The site can be accessed by two streets, one on the top level and another on the lower level.

The project fully unfolds on the first floor. Before the entrance, located in the center of the floor plan, there is a large courtyard with a parking lot as a pergola and access to the services area. After crossing the threshold the different rooms are laid out: in the center and to the left are the common areas and to the right, the bedrooms. The corridor to these bedrooms is designed so that one wall opens onto the main entrance, with woodwork and wooden walls. The stone walls, alternating straight and curved lines, are features both on the interior and exterior of the home.

Water is once again an axis running through the house in different ways. It is featured as a pond at the entrance and continues through the exterior as a canal that runs between the stone walls of the main suite and living room. Eventually, it flows into a small pool that is an extension of the bathroom suite, ending in the large infinity pool. Outside lounge areas with pergolas and a solarium were designed. On level −1 and at the other end of the site there is an apartment designed for guests.

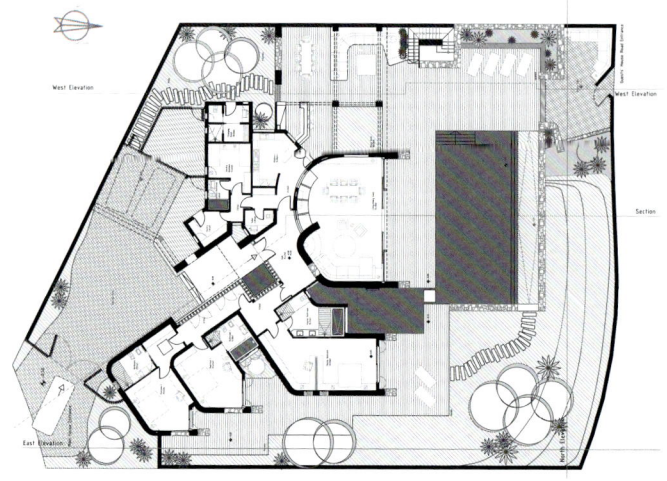

General plan

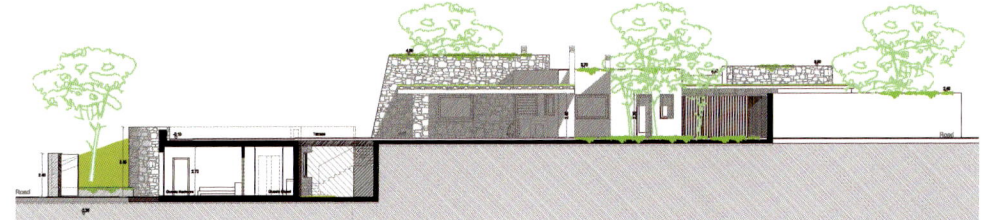

Sections

Model

DUNMOW HOUSE

Athens, Greece // 2009

 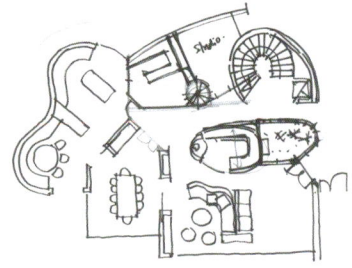 

Preliminary sketches

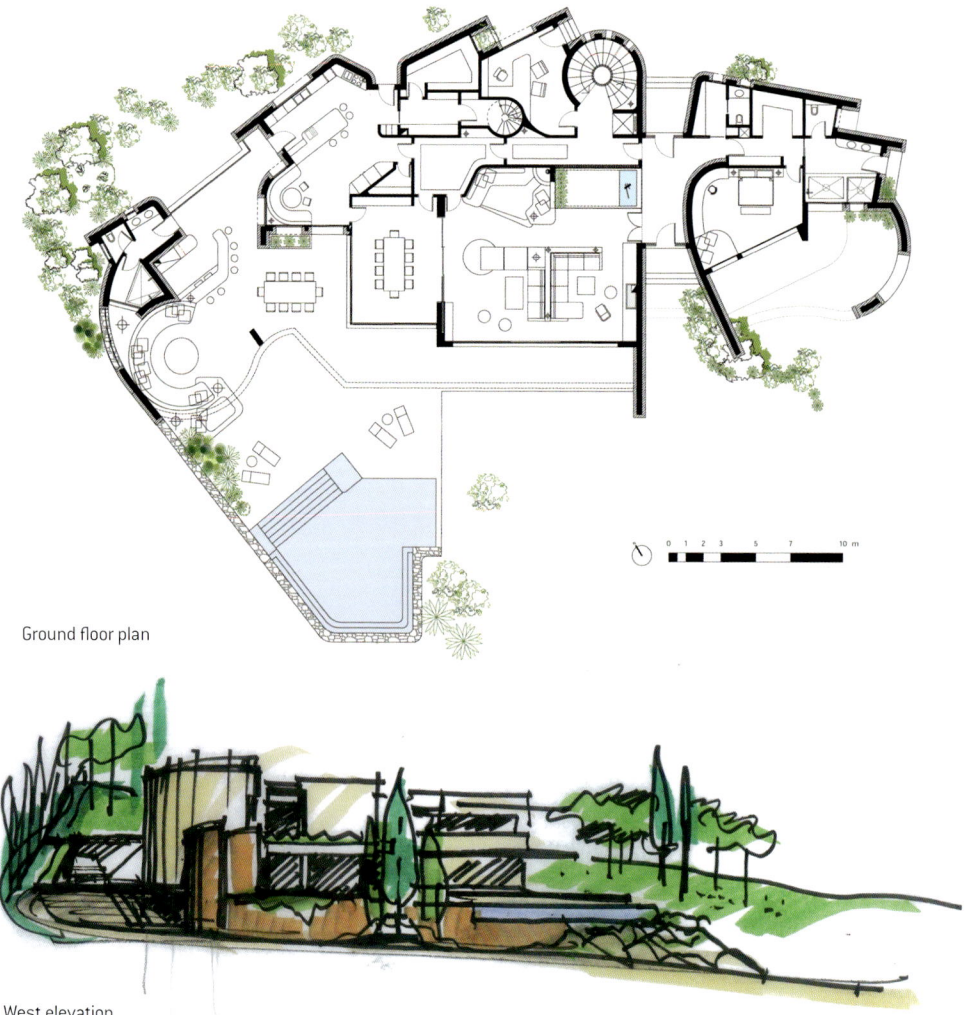

Ground floor plan

West elevation

This family home, located in the suburb of Kifissia, north of Athens, comprises three floors: basement, first and second floors. The topography of the site, crammed with tall pines, permits you to enjoy views over the surrounding hills, the Greek capital and the sea.

The house, located to the rear of the lot, has a linear approach in terms of the façade to better maximize the orientation and use of free space. It has two accesses: front for guests and rear for daily use. The path for vehicles veers to one side of the site to access the rear of the house. This path forms part of the garden's structure, with green paving stones that slow down the vehicle circulation and integrate it into the landscape.

The idea of respecting the privacy of the spaces in their indoor-outdoor relationship is a constant in the project. Following this premise, the guest room, on the first floor, is structured independently from the rest of the house, while the master bedroom also enjoys an intimate space. This feeling is achieved by straight stone walls, which are strong, and curved ones that embrace or mold the exterior space, volumes that move back and forth, and the different types of terraces. From a frontal perspective, the volume of the building is more concentrated to the right, taking a porch with a curved roof as a counterpoint. Stone and concrete are the basic materials, distributed according to usage, orientation and hierarchies. On the sheltered or rear side stone is predominant; except for wood used in the entrance while on the opposite side large wooden structures and a more balanced use of different materials stands out. A heated indoor pool and another summer pool complete the program for this home.

KANTARZOPOULOS HOUSE

Mykonos, Greece // 1999

This holiday home for a family from Athens is located on the island of Mykonos, on a site overlooking the isthmus. The design of this project was based on Estudio BC's principles: concern for the preservation of natural features, integrating the architecture into its surroundings and with these conditions the leitmotiv of the proposal emerged. The site was a challenge owing to its topography, with a 50% slope towards the sea, access from the top and a considerable number of rock groupings that cross the site diagonally. The views and good orientation fuse together to balance the situation. The building and outdoor areas were located on the flattest part of the site. The house has three storeys that form successive terraces. Two large double height side walls that follow the silhouette of the building and contain the different storeys were designed to protect the house. The plan includes a lower floor with guest bedrooms, a first floor with living areas and the top floor with the master bedrooms.

In an area bordered by rocks on the first floor, an outdoors space that has a pool and a solarium was designed. The main volume of the first floor is isolated and separated by a courtyard with the service area and the porch, which are partly embedded in a rock wall. The lower part of the land is connected by a passageway with steps that connects different levels and creates consecutive terraces. The materials used in this project include local stone, white plaster and woodwork the same color as the walls.

Preliminary sketches

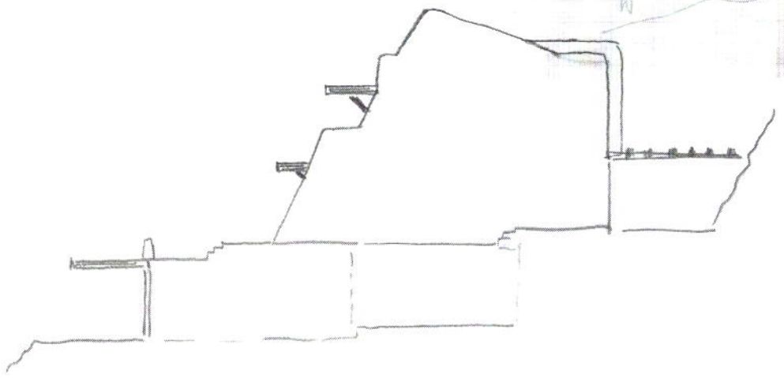

Section

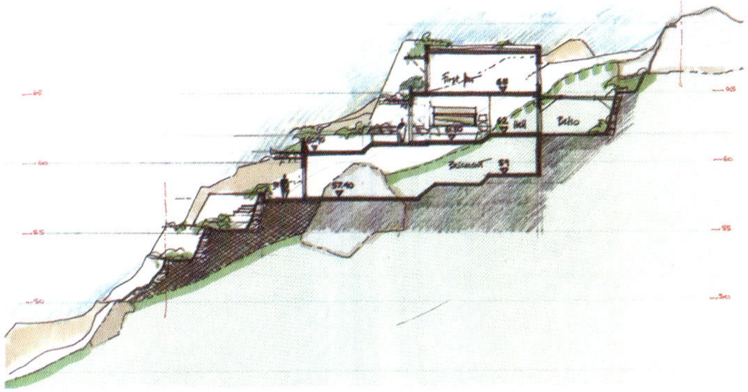

Section

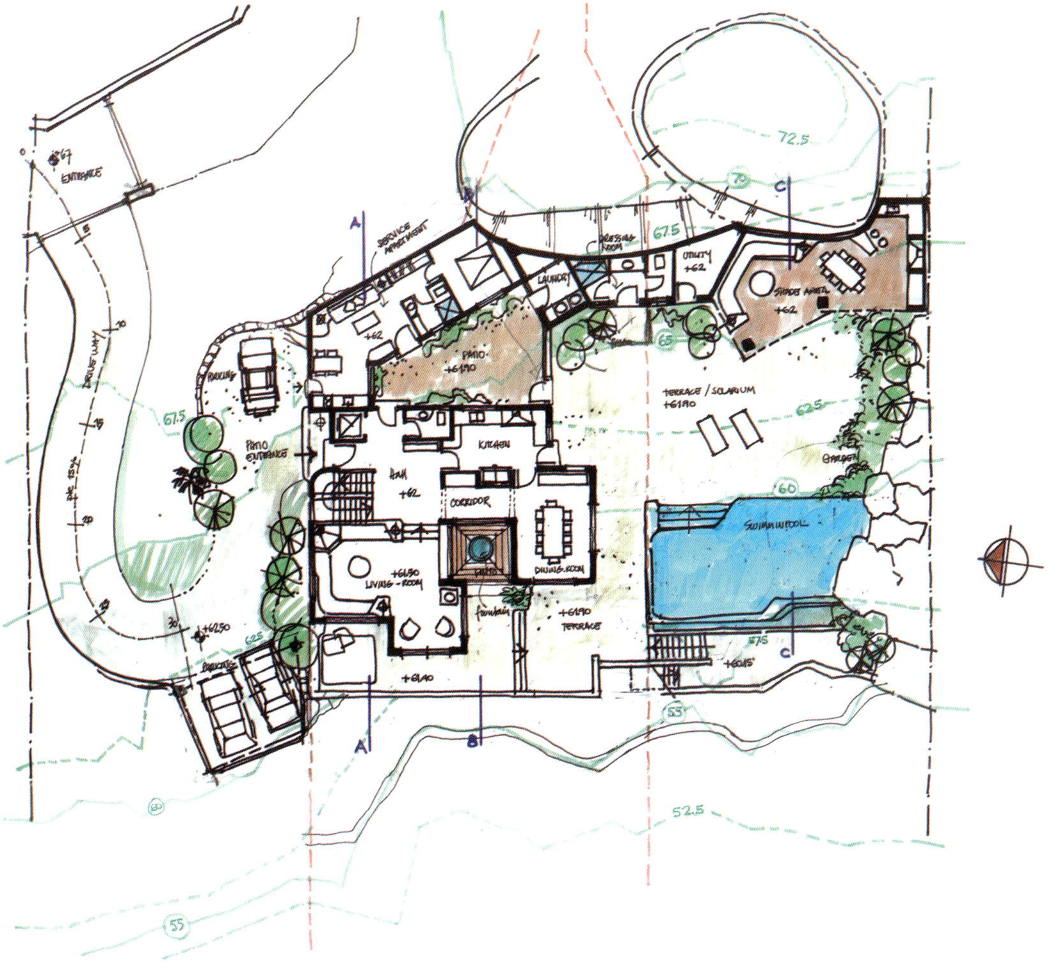

General plan

Elevations

KANTARZOPOULOS HOUSE // 135

HOUSE IN RODOPOLI

Athens, Greece // 2009

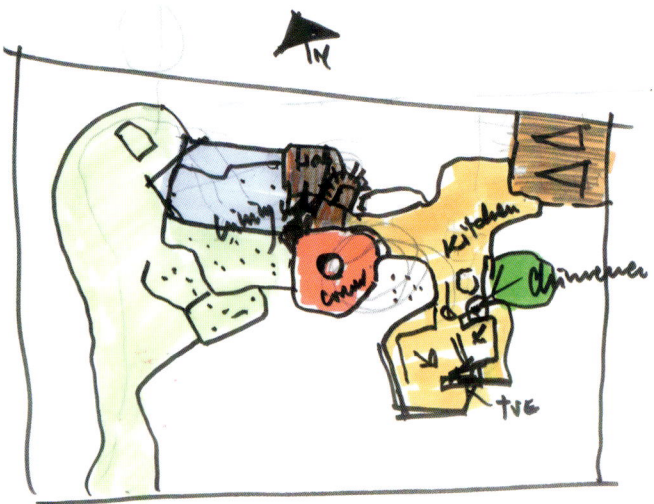

Preliminary sketches of the plan

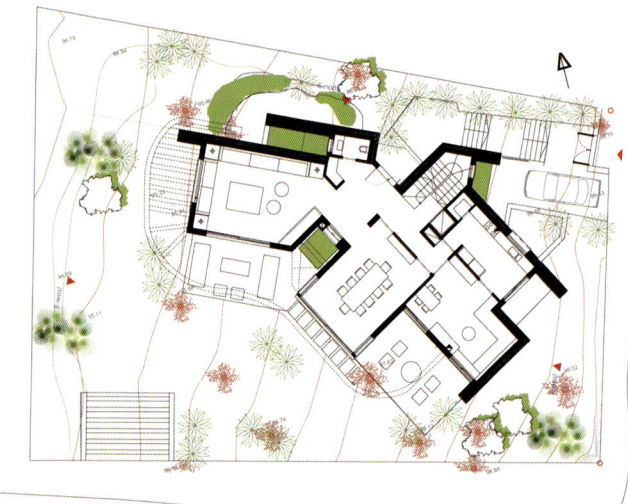

Ground floor plan

This detached house is located in a residential neighborhood of Athens, on a site surrounded by pine trees. For the owners it was essential to have a large garden. For this reason, the building was given a trapezoidal shape and erected on the northeastern side of the site, so as to achieve the best possible orientation. Access on foot leads to the central part of the house, which serves as the hub of circulation.

In the basement is the garage, plant room and service area. The house also includes a games room and an en suite guestroom, both of which receive natural light and ventilation through adjoining courtyards. On the ground floor is the living room, main dining room and a family area consisting of the kitchen, dining area and TV room. At the end of the garden, there is an area that was designed with terraces, duplicating the living and dining areas outdoors, underneath a porch running the length of the ground floor. The upper floor includes the main suite, with three bedrooms and two bathrooms at the other end. Beneath the sloping roof on the third floor there is the gym and study area.

The requirements of the family are wide-ranging and are organized on three different levels. So as to unify the overlap in activities, there is a large overhanging porch with curved forms, with railing or planters, depending on the area, providing a large border. These «bands» of concrete contain the penetrating and protruding volumes of the house.

Sustainable elements were used in this project, which was designed to maximize the use of natural resources, with excellent orientation, cross ventilation and areas of shade. It also includes a water tank to collect rainwater for recycling, and solar panels on the roof to provide hot water and heating. The materials used include stone, concrete and whitewash.

VAN VEGGEL HOUSE

Cascais, Portugal // 1999

Preliminary sketches

Built on top of a hill overlooking the Cabo da Roca and the Atlantic Ocean, and adjacent to the natural park of Guincho, this property was developed in keeping with feng shui. The entrance to the 64,583 sq ft triangular lot is a large gate that leads down a paved road bordered by vegetation and existing trees. The building unfolds on both sides of the wedge formed by the stone walls flanking the entrance, with a courtyard in the free space between the two wings. An organic corridor links the rooms, which open up like a fan to the incredible views. The building volume consists of two levels: first floor and basement. The first floor includes the living and dining areas to one side of the entrance, and the bedroom area to the other. This level ends with a suite, which via the outside flight of steps leads to the gym and pool area, located on the lower level. The basement contains the garage and other spaces.

The two-dimensional volume design that characterizes this house, with gravel or green roofs, is elevated at both ends of the building with pitched roofs, which increase the space in the rooms located directly below: the living room and master bedroom. Pergolas are used as protection from the summer sun, while the courtyards and pool areas provide shelter from cold northerly winds with a sundeck bordered by a semicircular pebble rock garden 20 ft high. In this area, olive trees stand as sculptures and the pool, with an irregular stone bottom, simulates a natural pond. The highlights of this project are the colored plasters, carpentry, flooring and wooden pergolas as well as the walls and floors of local stone.

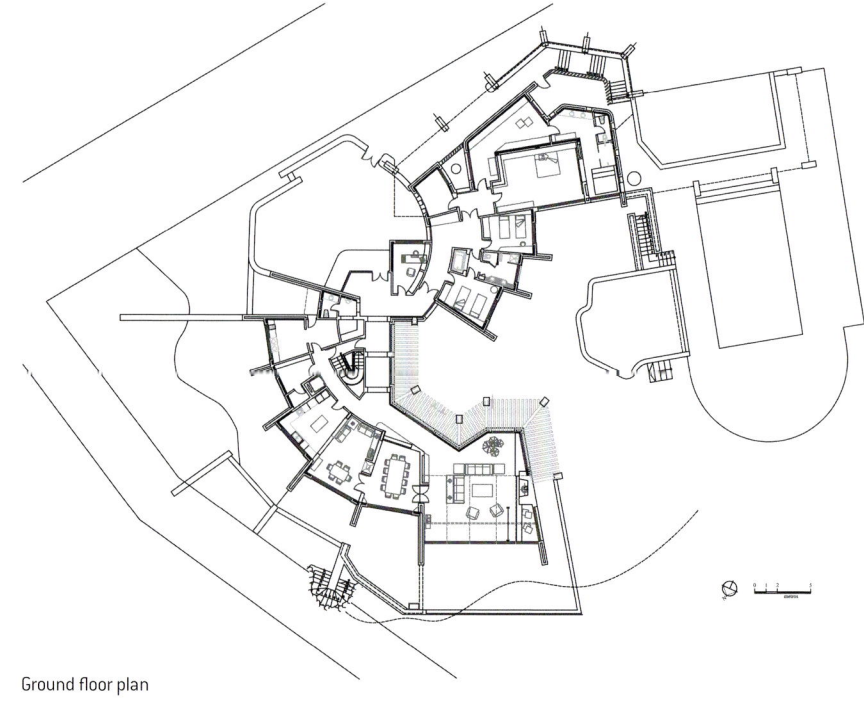

Ground floor plan

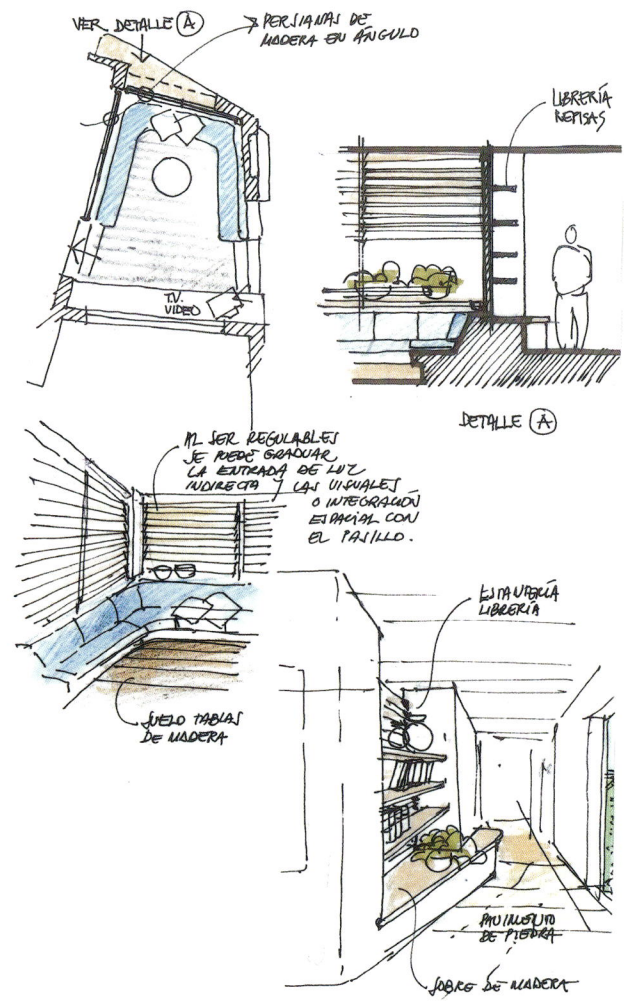

Study of interior spaces

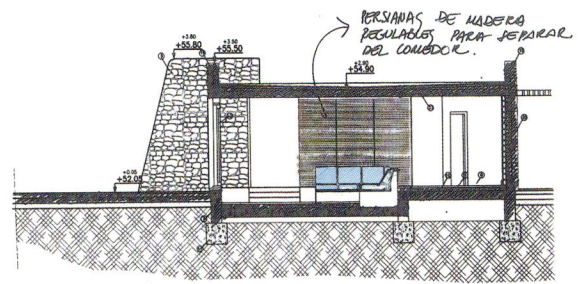

FACHADA
ESC. 1:100

CHALETS IN PINHAL VELHO

Vilamoura, Portugal // 2001

Land subdivision

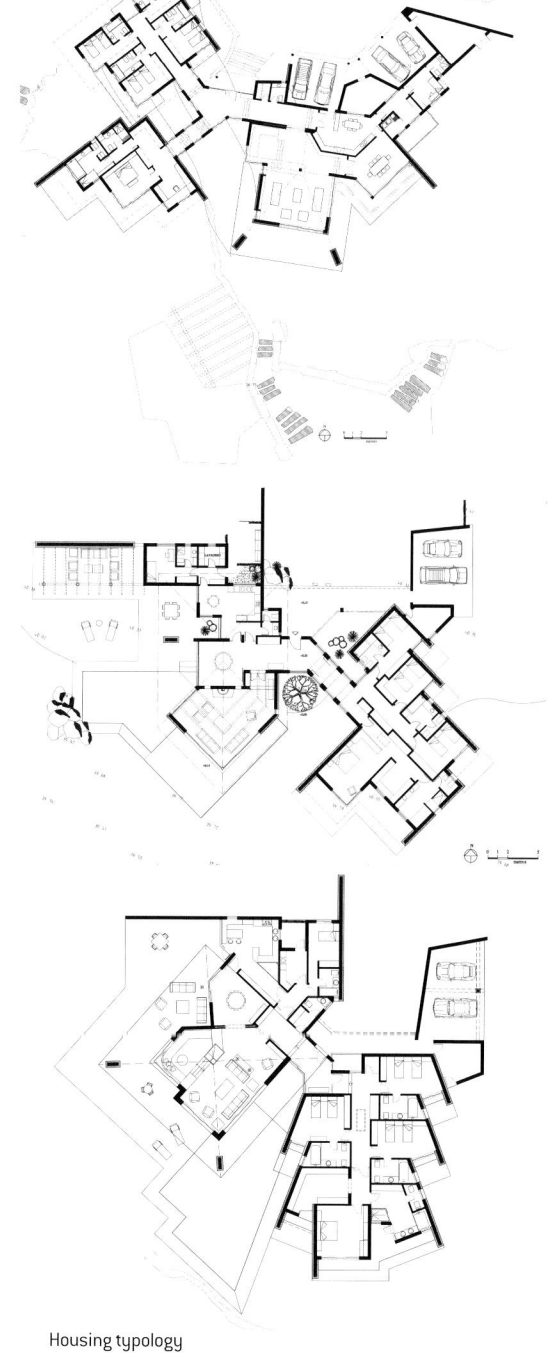

Housing typology

The Jordan family, whose company has developed top quality constructions over the years in Portugal, commissioned the project of 60 homes within the Pinhal Velho development and golf course, in a privileged landscape. During the project Estudio BC worked closely with Gilberto Jordan to take care of their concerns and to employ his knowledge on environmental issues and his professionalism.

Three types of houses were constructed, lots between 4,305 and 6,458 sq ft lots and between 43,055 and 53,819 sq ft. The program includes a living area, indoor and outdoor dining area, four en suite bedrooms, master bedroom, service area, gym, pool and parking lot.

In all the houses, an outspread design over the site was adopted and for the first floor or middle levels according to the topography of each lot. From the hall, a large corridor was planned that organizes the different indoor and outdoor areas, which are alternated with intermediate courtyards and gardens.

Estudio BC also designed the common areas of the development and how the lots were delimited, using irregular perimeter fencing. These forms allow the existing trees on the path to be maintained, emphasizing the presence of natural elements.

The project was subject to regulations requiring some pitched roofs with tiles and other flat roofs. This was used as a resource in the structure of the houses, working with pitched roofs with wooden structures over the living areas, library and dining room. The flat roofs were designed at different heights, lower at the entrance and corridors, and higher in bedrooms and other rooms. The stone walls and floors and textured plaster in warm tones are prominent features.

GREENLANDIA

St. Petersburg, Russia // 2004

General plan

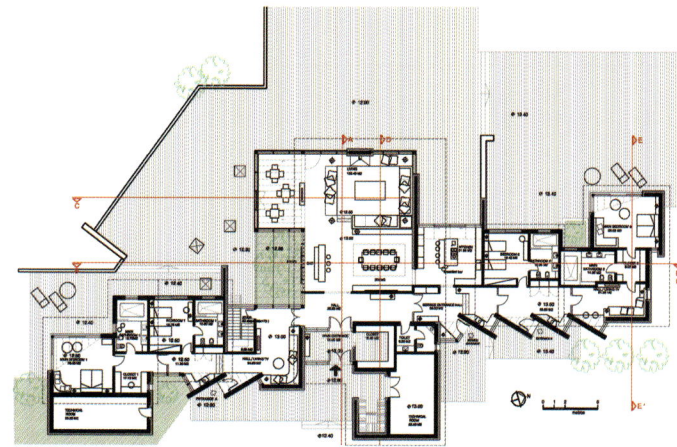

Ground floor plan of the family and guest house

The site of this project is located on the shores of Lake Bolshoe Borkovo, 31 miles from St. Petersburg, surrounded by gentle slopes and a thick pine forest. The project, at the express request of the client, consists of a house for himself and another for the rest of the family. Because of the size of the lot, a walkway connects the different areas. In the access, a services house was planned, attached to the outer wall that encloses the site.

The owner's house is located on the shores of the lake, and includes a sauna-house connected to it. The volume is organized around a central pentagonal loft-type space, around a large fireplace and a spacious veranda enabling the home to expand outwards in the summer. The bedrooms are to one side of the house and to the other, the sauna-house. This is arranged following Nordic criteria: a small pool, showers, sauna and a lounge. Its proximity to the lake means that the ritual can be completed by plunging into icy waters.

The family and guest house has two floors, with common areas in the center and two wings with bedroom suites. Both levels are only partially visible from the front of the building as terraces were built to make use of the uneven land.

At the rear, where you can access the building, there is a hill that hides the volume making it emerge from the land. This feeling is strengthened by using local materials (wood and stone) and copper roofs in the opposite direction to the lake, to make the most of natural light with large windows.

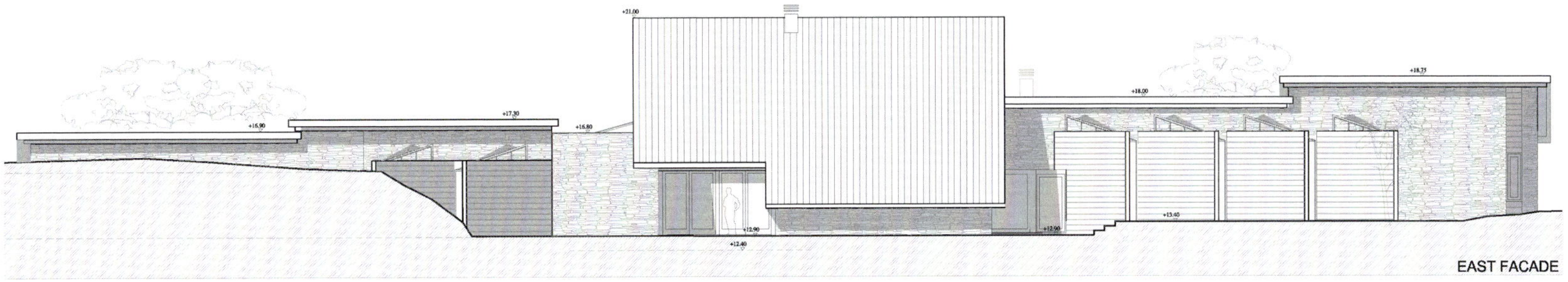

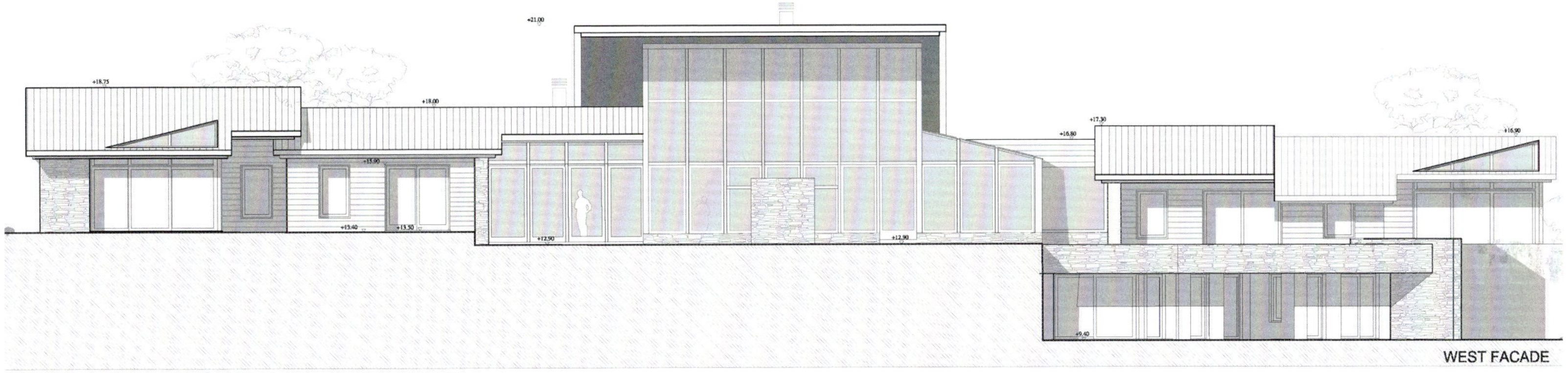

Perspectives

GREENLANDIA // 147

APARTMENT IN ST. PETERSBURG

St. Petersburg, Russia // 2005

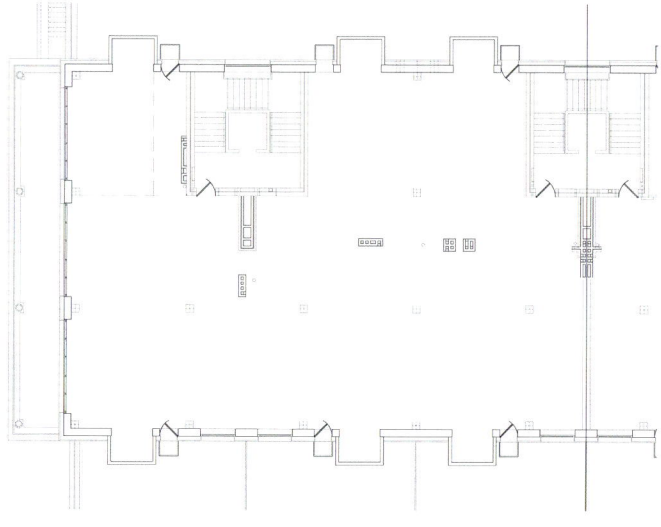

Existing floor plan

The main objective of this project was the union of two apartments in a newly built lakefront building, which the client had purchased to create a larger surface area. A new distribution of spaces within the existing empty structure was planned. Divisions between the new environments are straight or curved, avoiding the use of conventional doors. A succession of wooden vertical elements define the corridor which breaks up the structure of a conventional floor and become a leitmotif that identifies the different areas. Sliding doors formed of double-glazed glass with sheets of natural stone barely a few millimeters thick inserted in the middle are also fitted between the living room and the suite. The passageway is designed as an axis that makes a statement owing to its winding and undulating lines, combining noble materials such as stone and wood or wood and copper. Half of the apartment, including the kitchen, the dining-living room and the master bedroom, was designed as a loft. This space features water elements, such as the large fish tank that is built into one of the walls, and fire elements, such as the majestic fireplace placed between the living room and the dining room area. Vegetation is also an important element of the project, and the walls of the two balconies were designed as small greenhouses. In the other half of the area, a study area, two bedroom suites and another kitchen and a laundry room with independent access are located.

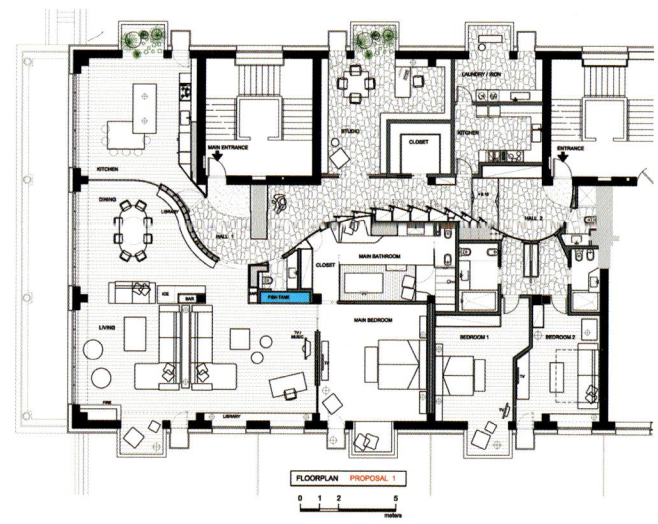

Proposed floor plan

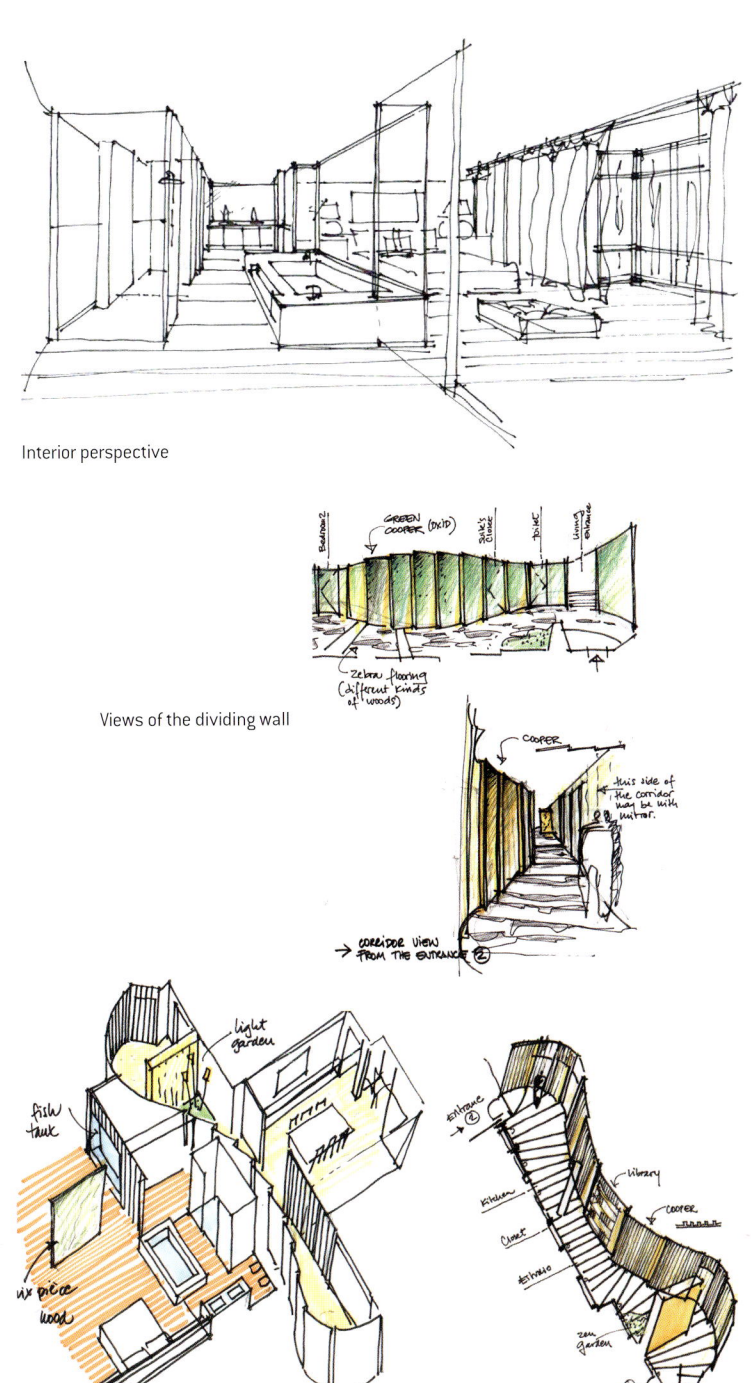

Interior perspective

Views of the dividing wall

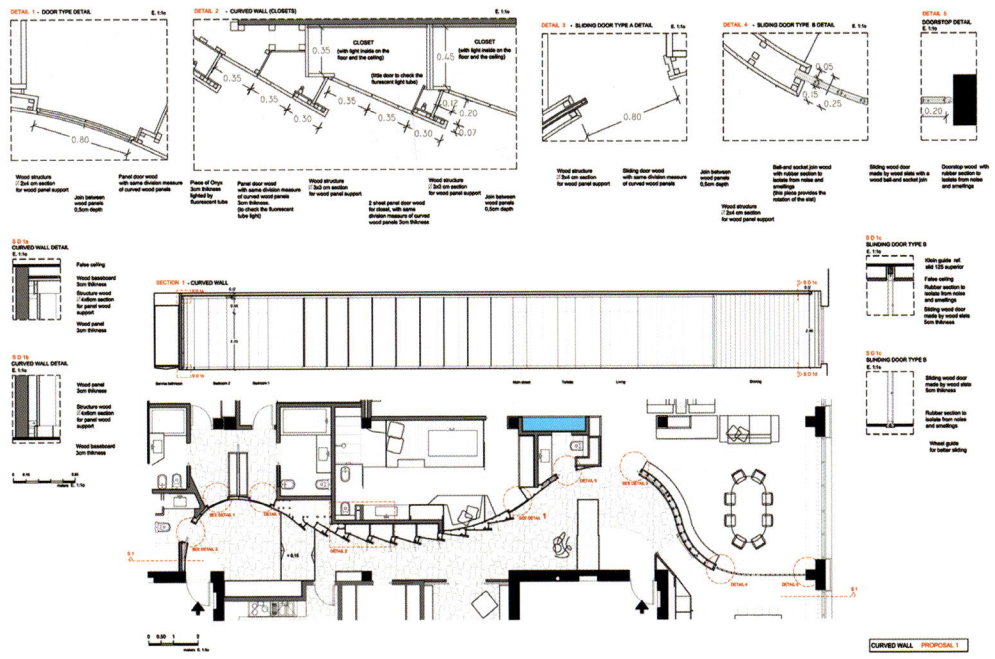

Detail of the dividing wall in the hallway

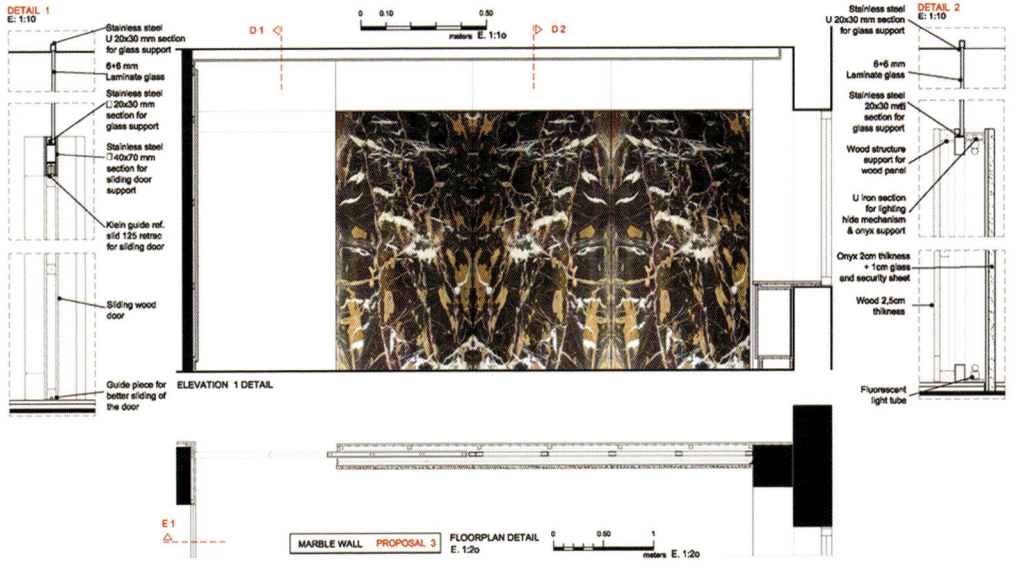

Separation wall detail

APARTMENT IN ST. PETERSBURG

HUNEEUS HOUSE

Napa Valley, California, USA // 2000

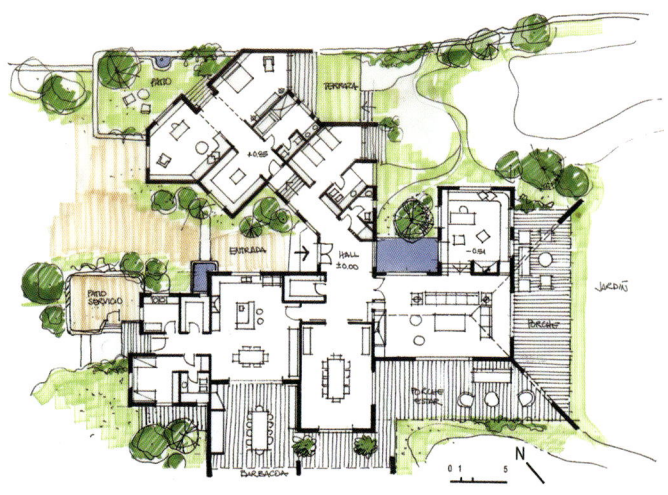

Floor plan

The house project for the owners of Quintessa winery in Napa Valley, California, is located in a privileged place within the estate. The long, narrow site, shaped like a wedge, boasts the best views of the vineyards and is surrounded by many mature oak trees.

A stone wall defines the site, which is accessed through a large portal that connects a road to the center of the lot. The different buildings are distributed around this point, with free spaces throughout: the gatehouse leads to the main house on a lower level which includes a swimming pool, a solarium and a porch.

The entrance to the main house, located in the middle, is flanked by linear, diagonally-arranged stone walls. Upon entering the house, you can see both the outdoor spaces, the pond and the landscape, and the interior spaces: the living room with a fireplace, library, study and guest room. The other rooms are laid out to the sides, hidden behind the walls flanking the entrance. To the southwest there is a kitchen and an open dining-living area, with a wood porch that acts as a pergola on the outside. To the southeast, there is a guest bedroom and a suite which includes a meditation area. Stone walls are a feature throughout the project; there are a variety of rectangular, triangular and screening walls that make up the volume of the main house. This complex, which is built amid a mature oak wood, is clearly defined by these walls, but also by the strong volumes in painted deep warm colors with pitched roofs that gradually descend to the ground.

House access

General perspective

Section NW-SE

GIROD HOUSE

Baja California, Mexico // 2000

Perspectives

The location of this house is a unique unspoilt coastal vacation spot in Baja California, on top of an arid hill, dotted with cacti and other xerophytic species characteristic of the area, with stunning views of the sea and the surrounding landscape. The isolated house is accessed via a road that widens to allow parking under pergolas. After crossing a courtyard with two imposing, colorful walls, you arrive at the house. The same courtyard forms a microclimate that allows for a garden with a variety of species.

The house has a linear approach. The rooms are located in the interior including a large living room-dining room designed on a slope and crowned with a large 'palapa', a typical Mexican structure built of palm fronds.

Exterior inclined walls separate the rooms of the house. This architectural resource offers the rooms privacy, while, due to their simplicity and force, strengthen the presence of the house on the site. Harmony with the environment is achieved through the use of earth tones and rustic textures in these walls, as well as the form of the house in general, which provides a visual symbiosis with the landscape.

As a counterpoint to the elements that integrate the house with the environment, the inside treatment of the rooms, designed by the artist Toni Agustí, is a chromatic explosion: a mix of intense red or blue, which are reminiscent of the Mexican culture that permeates this land.

LA ISLA VERDE©

Barcelona, Spain // 1992

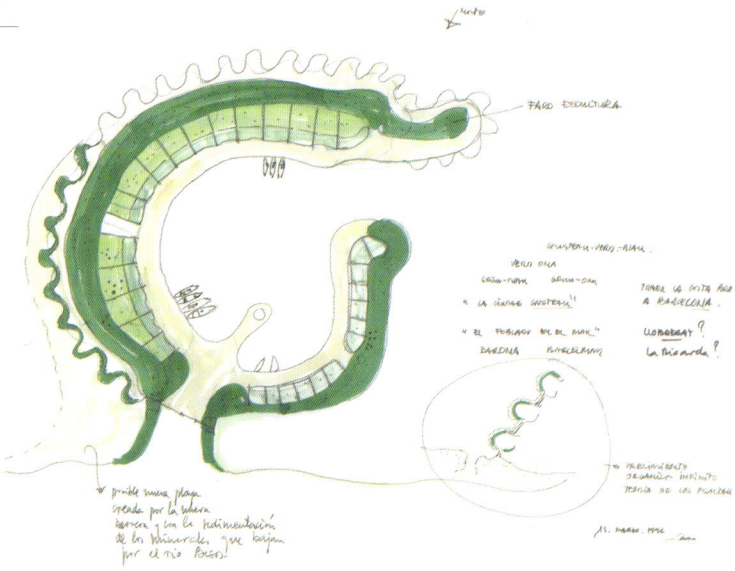

La Isla Verde© is a self-contained urban community, in spite of being designed on reclaimed land; it was to be built on a rock foundation that generates a biotype for marine life, as well as human occupation.

The project is planned for the coast of Barcelona, although due to its characteristics the model is perfectly applicable to any coastal area around the world. The community includes 344,445.133 sq ft for 202 bioclimatic houses, which make full use of the existing resources, reducing energy consumption – 1,02257.148 sq ft are planned for private gardens and 164,580.190 sq ft for parking lots, located on the wooded hillside that surrounds the complex. In addition, 20,989.625 sq ft are projected for shops, a hotel, a spa, a marina, bars, and restaurants, as well as 147,465.572 sq ft for promenades and a beach.

On La Isla Verde©, it is worth mentioning the use of efficient energy both in homes and in the half-buried public spaces. The use of renewable energy, such as wind, solar and geothermal, is paramount. It also treats and recycles gray water to irrigate the Mediterranean vegetation on the island. Traffic on the island is limited to electric vehicles as the circulation of fuel-driven vehicles is prohibited.

This project was included in the exhibition *Il·luminacions. Catalunya Visionària* (Illuminations. Visionary Catalonia), produced by the Barcelona Contemporary Culture Center (CCCB) with support from the Departament de Cultura i Mitjans de Comunicació de la Generalitat de Catalunya, organized in 2009. It also received the support of Greenpeace, as an example of sustainable development.

Location on the coastline of Barcelona near the mouth of the Besòs River

Perspective

Section

Schematic section

From drawing to model

General model

Next page:
1. Bridge access from the city
2. Apartments and lighthouse
3. Port entrance
4. Island and marina

158 // RESIDENTIAL COMPLEXES

1

2

3

4

LA ISLA VERDE © // 159

PREDIO DE SA FÚA

Minorca, Spain // 1998

Cross section

Predio de Sa Fúa is a unique residential complex in one of the most beautiful areas in the south of Minorca. The complex consists of 36 bioclimatic houses surrounded by vegetation. These are divided into four rows each with nine houses, following the natural slope of the land that descends to the sea in terraces. This distribution enables all households to enjoy the views, as the terraces are on the upper level and are slightly elevated above the roof garden of the housing directly below. The complex faces south to get more sunlight. The use of thermal clay brick, stone cladding on the walls and landscaped roofs produce major energy savings, while integrating the houses into the landscape. The use of the excavated rocks to build the walls of the property allows for maximum integration with the natural landscape.

Local vegetation —Mediterranean plants, shrubs and trees— can be seen in both public and private spaces. The green roofs regulate the temperature inside. The pools are integrated into the houses, so that from the interior they look like sheets of water that can be confused with the sea.

This project is a good example of the fact that the sophistication of exclusive homes is not incompatible with bioclimatic architecture and careful landscape design, and that the aesthetics need not be incompatible with a sustainable home. In 2002 the Promaris European Mediterranean Foundation awarded the complex the First Prize for Mediterranean Environmental Quality, which recognizes the efforts in environmental conservation and sustainable development.

Aerial view of the site

18 HOUSES IN AIGUABLAVA

Begur, Spain // 2003

General plan

Next page:
Photomontage of the development

After studying the program for the housing, the land topography and urban conditions, the studio designed two rows of houses with their respective access roads: one higher on the western boundary of the site and another lower down on the site. The general access is in the far southeast. From this point, an ascending road connects the two streets leading to the rows of houses.

To overcome the irregularity of the land four types of houses were developed. Each home has an individual access and the site includes a car park space under a pergola. In addition, garages were placed under the slope of the land and with roof gardens, so that they will not be noticed.

All the houses have two wings separated by a hall with a sea view: one for the common areas and kitchen-utility rooms, and the other for the bedroom suites. The living-dining room sector boasts wide exterior porches, with canopies. The pool and terrace-garden area complete the house. The slopes are maintained by stone walls or rock gardens and plants to form the main terrace. The architectural concept of the houses demands sea views from all rooms and the integration with the garden, as well as the establishment of courtyards to separate the rooms.

The construction is characterized by the traditional system of weight-bearing walls and slabs of prestressed beams. Emphasis is on natural elements such as stone and wood floors, planted rooftops, and heather-shaded porches.

166 // RESIDENTIAL COMPLEXES

Photomontage

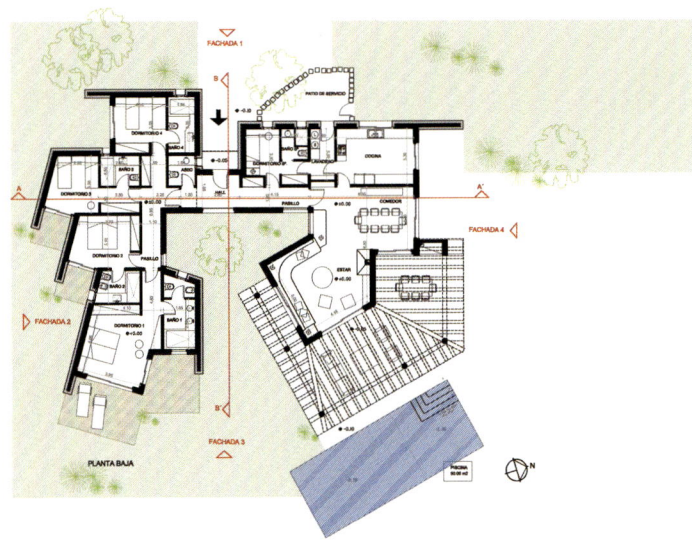

Dwelling plan type A

Dwelling plan type B

VILLAGE IN SANT MORI

Sant Mori, Spain // 1998

The maxim of this project was to integrate the new residential complex into the existing medieval urban layout of the village of Sant Mori. The program consisted of 68 houses, five of them isolated in lots of between 16,145 and 21,527 sq ft and the other 63 semi-detached houses in lots of between 1,291 and 4,843 sq ft with commercial and social facilities.

The architectural and urban development arose from the idea of respecting the characteristics of the landscape and using the most characteristic elements of the town, such as its urban design, streets and housing types as a reference point.

The road structure was designed from the topographic study. It includes part of the existing roads and gives access to different areas of the complex. The green space and isolated lots are located to the far northeast of the site. As you leave the village of Sant Mori to the northwest a village road branches off in two directions, one following the main road, and the other becomes the Paseo de Agua, making use of an existing stream.

Green spaces are present throughout the project, both in courtyards and gardens in the homes and also in larger-scale plazas and groves. In order to respect the local elements and not to break the visual harmony, the whole landscape was designed using native vegetation species.

A noteworthy element of this residential complex is the application of sustainable resources such as solar panels for hot water for domestic use, photovoltaic cells for street lighting and sewage treatment by biological treatment processes. This set of characteristics enabled the project to register in the EU Joule-Thermie program for energy use, endorsing bioclimatic architecture.

General view

Axonometric view of the square

Study of the square

VILLAGE IN SANT MORI // 171

VILLAGE ON PAROS ISLAND

Paros, Greece // 2002

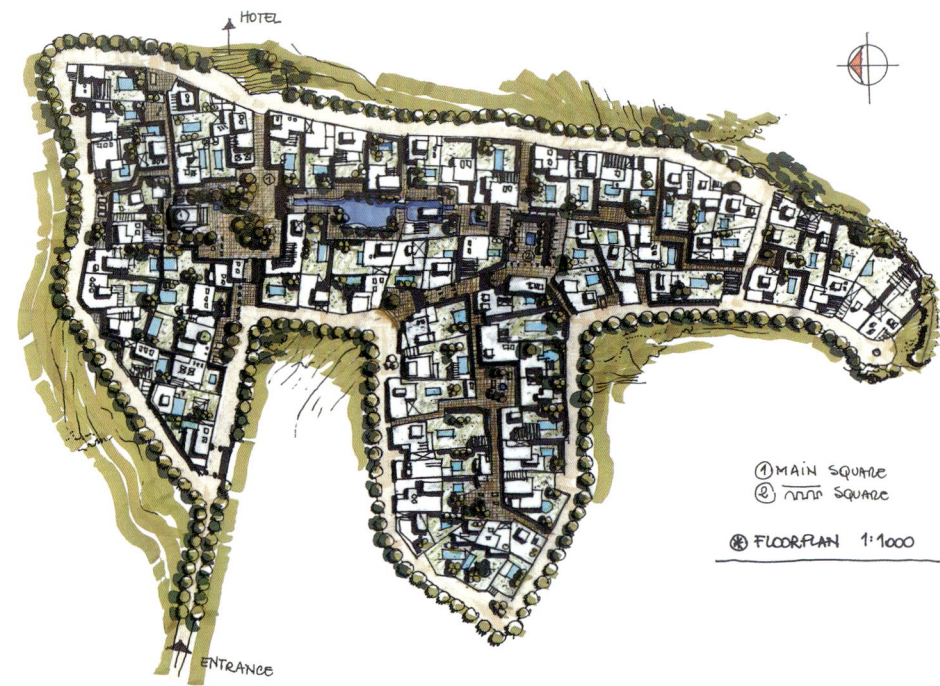

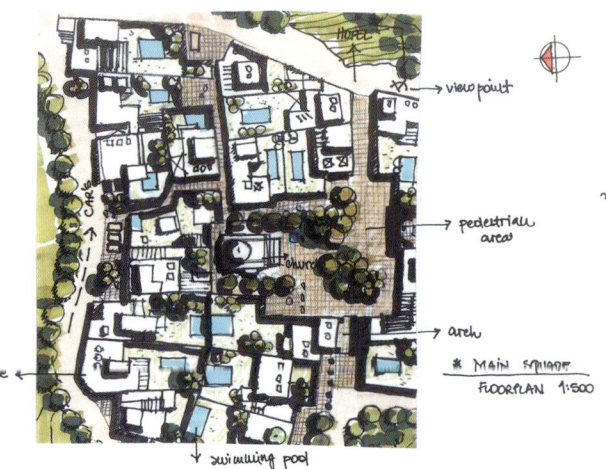

General plan and detail

The non-invasive and ecological philosophy that Estudio BC transmits in all its work coincided from the outset with the objective of this project, a comission that was presented to the studio by the Greek developer N. Zefkilis. The idea was to create a settlement on the island of Paros, the third largest of the Cyclades archipelago.

The strict urban regulations, aimed at preserving the vernacular architecture of the island, favored the creative process instead of curtailing the inspiration for the development of the proposal. The geography, the totally irregular lie of the land and the requirements of the developer were all added to the above determining factors.

The settlement is structured like a small town: a perimetral, circulatory structure and two major axes that make up the maximum length and width of the land. From here, a stretch of narrow streets with restricted traffic interweaves different plazas – the main one with a small church and basic shops, and small squares, featuring vegetation and water features.

Given the irregularity of the land, the housing plots are all different, and so four types of residences were designed. Each is equipped with a small garden and a private pool. On some stucco façades, there are stairs leading to the roofs, which become viewing points. The aim of ensuring that all homes have good views had to overcome the limitation of height, as the law permits a first floor and one other level. This required the careful study of the distribution of the terraces and roofs to avoid invading privacy and at the same time, to enable a sea view above the town.

172 // RESIDENTIAL COMPLEXES

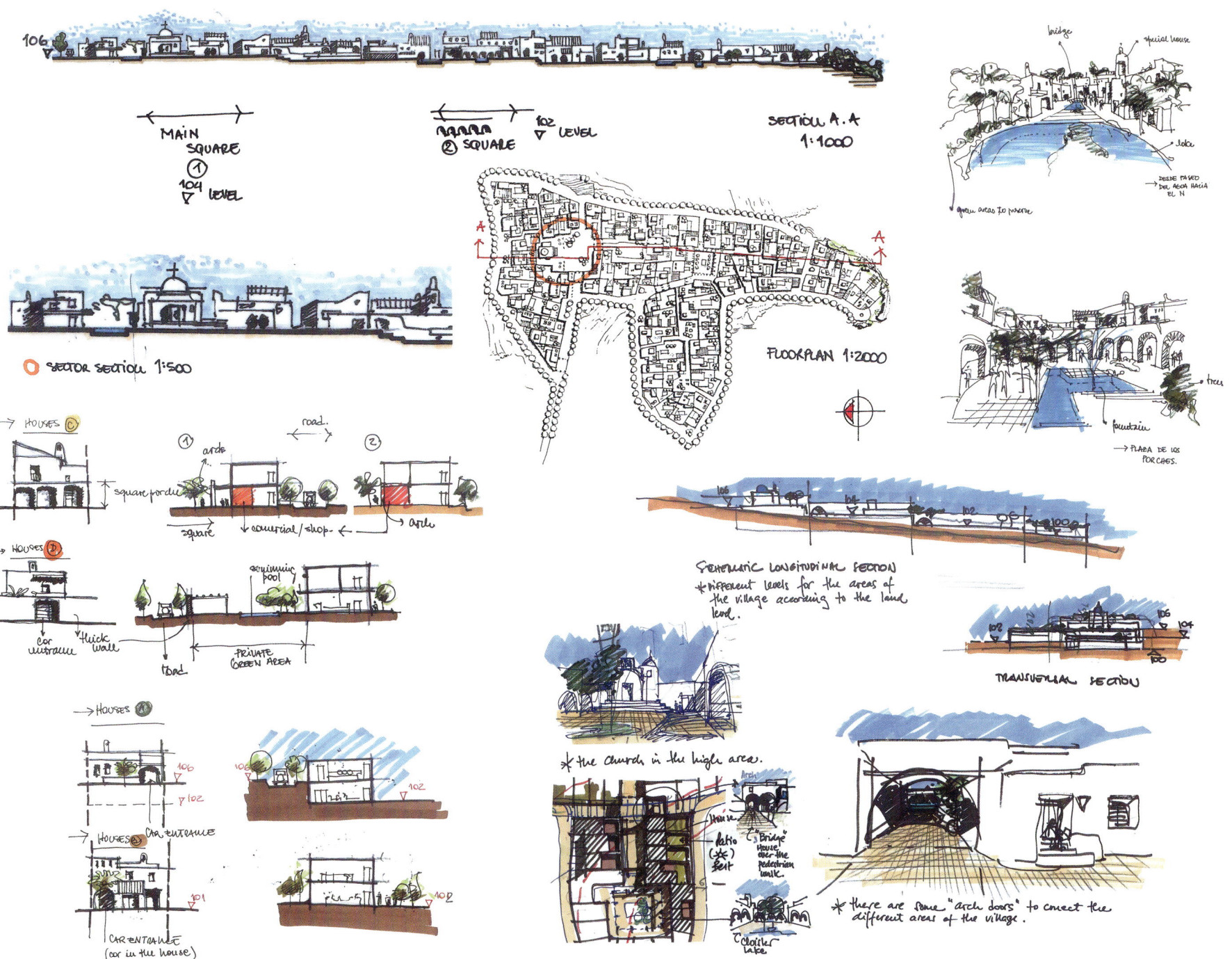

Dwelling and square typology study

HOUSES IN LIA

Mykonos, Greece // 2008

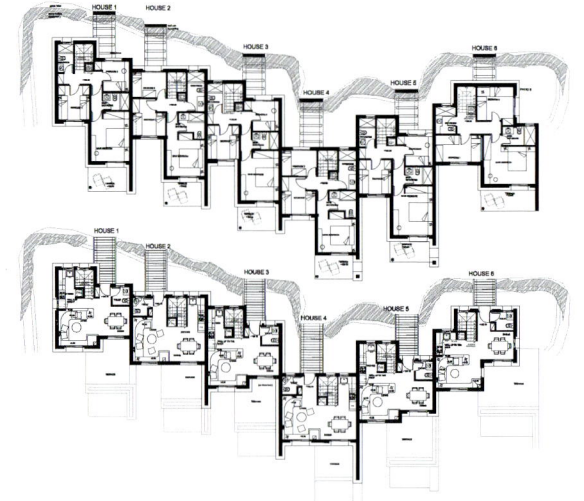

Ground floor and upper floor of the dwellings

This project of six small houses is developed on a large rectangular lot with excellent views over the Aegean Sea. The main entrance, which leads to the access road to the homes, sits on the northeast side of the site, which has steep topography to the north. At the end of this road, the parking lot is located under a pergola, with spaces for all properties.

The complex forms a row of houses arranged on three different levels that follows the topography. The volume of the complex stands out with its recesses and projections alternated with white stucco and stone walls in a harmonious contrast of tones and textures. Wood is also incorporated into these two basic materials, used in the carpentry, pergolas and porches. This careful selection allows the whole project to be seen as a heterogeneous unit, volumetrically inspired by vernacular architecture. Chimney sculptures that crown the roofs are also used.

Each of the homes also boasts terraces and pergolas. The first floor where the entrance is located houses the kitchen, a bathroom and the living room with a fireplace. On the lower floor, which is the natural ground level, there are three bedrooms and two bathrooms. The two houses at the ends of the row have a unique design because of their position. They have more outdoors space, including, a living-dining area and a small pool under a pergola.

BLACK STONE

Athens, Greece // 2009

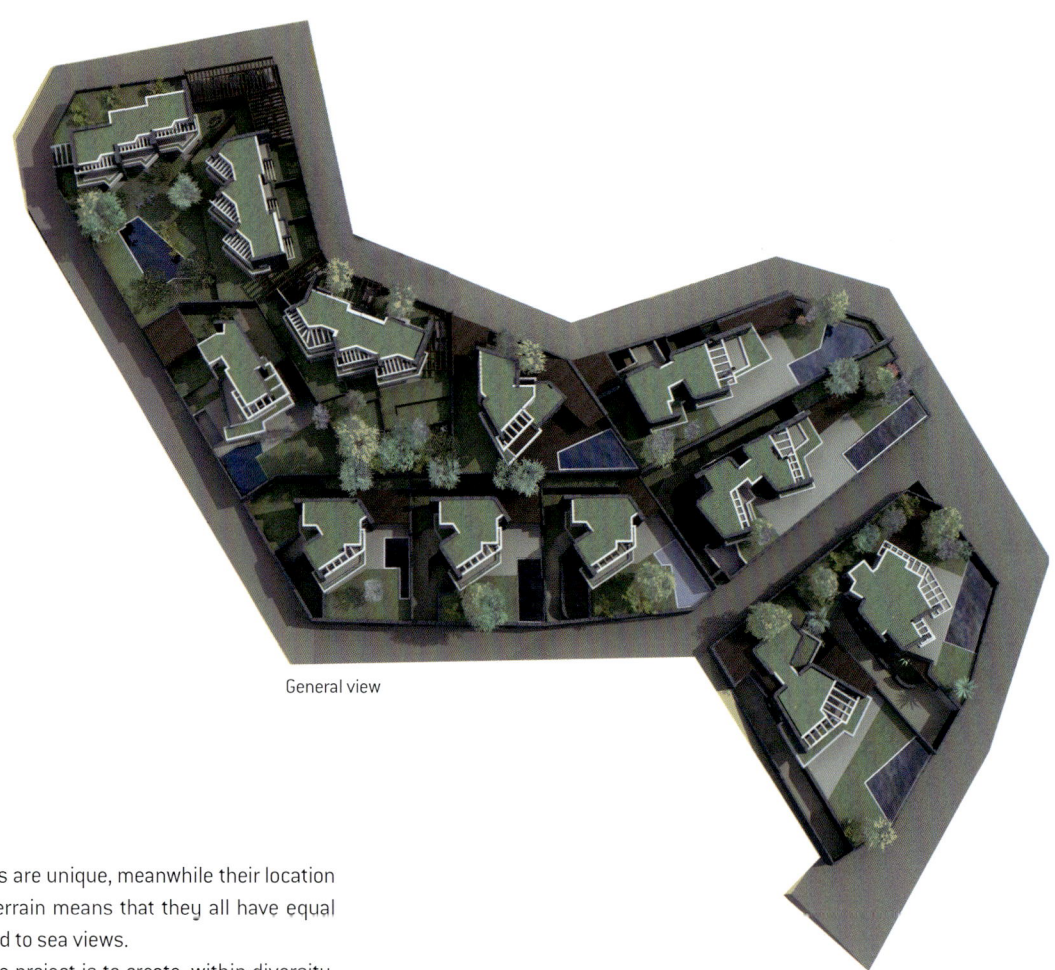
General view

This project takes its name from its location. The lot, with superb views, is located next to the road that borders the sea, between Athens and Cape Sounion.

The program includes dividing the land and designing nine apartments and a few other single-family houses. Due to factors such as the topography of the site, which has a slope towards the sea, the orientation and the search for the best views, Estudio BC proposed a varied division of lots.

Each unit works individually with its functional program and the conditions of the lot, without losing sight of its relation with the boundary and adjacent elements. The houses themselves are unique, meanwhile their location and level on the terrain means that they all have equal conditions in regard to sea views.

The idea behind the project is to create, within diversity, a unitary whole. Intentionally, the design sought to highlight the lines of the stone walls in the landscape that enclose the land and form the gardens. These walls also define the lots and alternate with the various volumes of the houses. The contrast of colors and texture from the combination of the dark stone volumes with white stucco reinforces this idea that permeates the complex.

HRH PRINCE SULTAN BIN FAHAD RED SEA RESIDENCE

Jeddah, Saudi Arabia // 2007

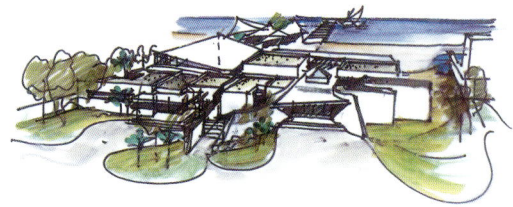

This complex is a private residential construction of 129,166 sq ft designed for the Saudi Arabian royal family. The project commissioned by HRH Princess Aljohara Bint Faisal Bin Turkei Bin Abdullah Al Saud, included the necessary buildings for the family. The client made the intelligent suggestion that the project was designed as a resort integrated into the site based on environmental criteria. The client's knowledge and great interest in architecture and interior design became apparent during the different stages of the project.

In the complex, family life is combined with receiving international personalities and friends and managing the activities of the members of the royal household. The distribution and size of spaces meet this need. A villa for the family, one for the prince, two for the daughters, one for direct employees and four guest houses, as well as a service area, security and outdoor areas were all planned. Privacy between buildings is achieved by their layout on the land along with the use of plants and curved walls. In the family villa a double-height hall and a spectacular staircase are prominent features. In the prince's house, the entrance turns into a courtyard-cloister. Both are situated by the Red Sea.

The structure of the complex is based around a two-lane main street with palm trees in the middle that connects the areas from the entrance to the private beach, with a pool in the sea, relaxation areas, wide avenues and a pier for fishing.

The weather conditions demanded that the setting was able to cope with high temperatures and sandstorms. Succulents were planted on the roofs and green slopes, while drought-resistant plants stand out in the landscaping.

Perspectives

General plan

Sections

Photograph of the model

HRH PRINCE SULTAN BIN FAHAD RED SEA RESIDENCE // 179

Photographs of the model

HRH PRINCE SULTAN BIN FAHD RED SEA RESIDENCE // 181

LUXURY RESORT HOTEL IN BOROBUDUR

Borobudur, Indonesia // 1993

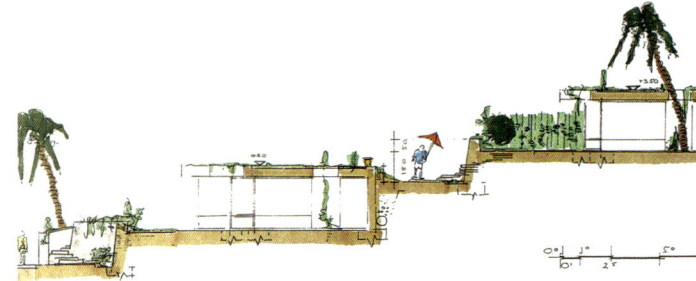

Typological section

The lush vegetation, rice fields and mountains of Central Java, in Indonesia offer the perfect setting for one of the wonders of the world: the world heritage Borobudur Buddhist temple. With over 1,100 years of history, this monument remains a sanctuary and place of pilgrimage for Buddhists.

Javier Barba was asked to design a luxury resort high on a hill overlooking the temple. The spirituality and the virginity of the landscape resulted in many great challenges for the studio, which was inspired by the topography of the land and the vernacular style of the location. The project is organized around the two existing rivers and the creation of a central water axis aligned with the temple of Borobudur. From this axis, different ponds and waterfalls emerge, which acoustically and visually enrich the common areas.

At the entrance, there is a large courtyard with walls made of local stone next to a bridge leading to different *pendopos*, typical Javanese constructions consisting of open rectangular pavilions supported on columns. The best views of the temple can be seen from the main *pendopo*.

The two rivers define the boundaries of the resort. The bungalows, which are partially buried, provide a clear view of the valley of the temples, and can be accessed via the crossroads of these watercourses. These bungalows disappear under green roofs, in a staggered sequence that integrates them into the existing rice terraces.

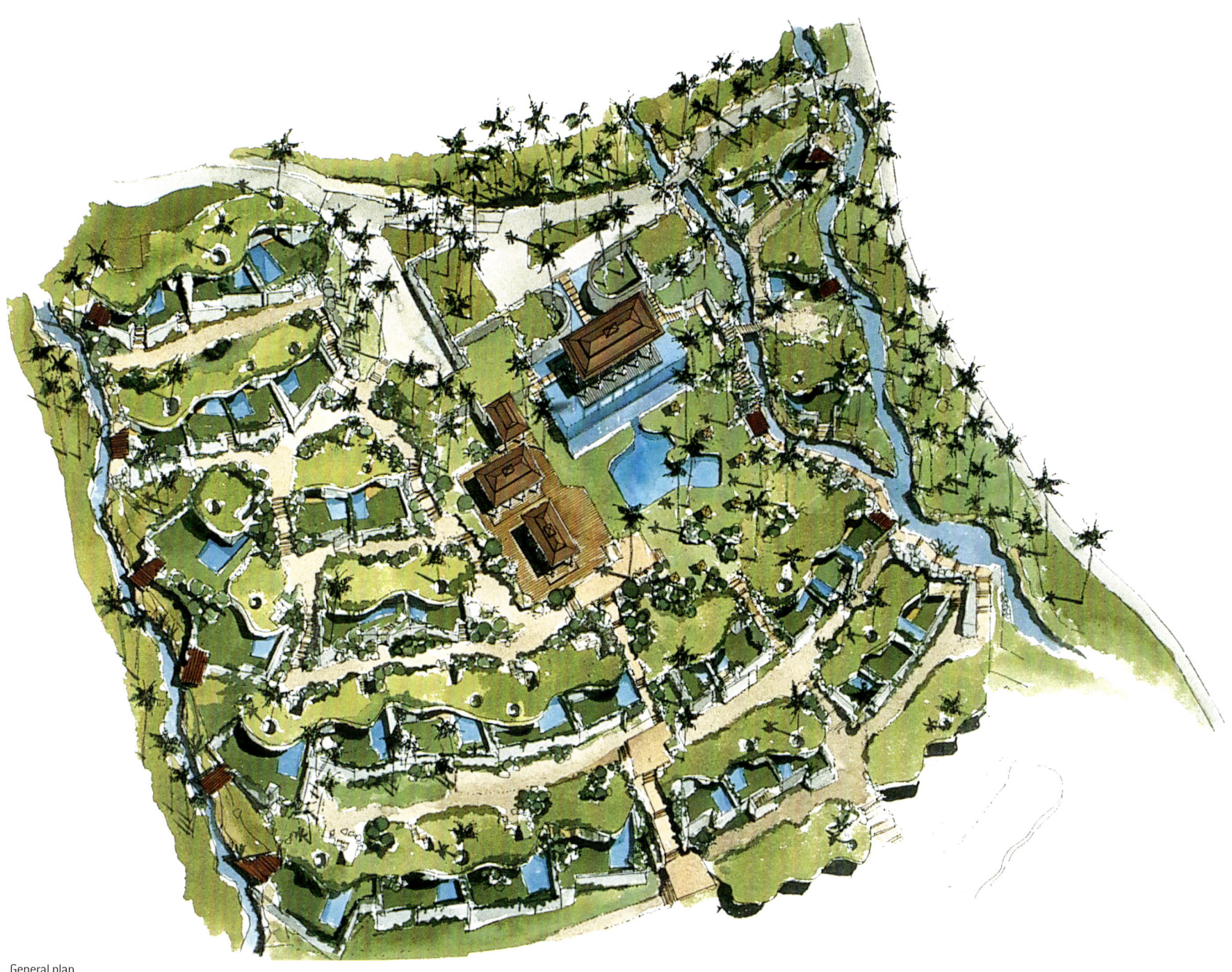
General plan

SAN BLAS VALLEY RESORT

Tenerife, Spain // 2000

This hotel complex situated in Playa San Blas has only one access from the highway, with two lateral parking lots. From this point onwards, only pedestrians and electrical transportation will be permitted. A courtyard entrance and a bridge lead to a large lobby from where visitors can access the reception halls of each of the hotels.

The complex is structured around a large water axis in the center of the site and perpendicular to the coast, which has its source in the lake that borders the reception area and ends in a recreation area with a pool overlooking the sea. Along its course, the water creates cascades and pools at different points of the site. One of the bars and various amenities for guests can also be found in this central axis.

Parallel to the water feature, the hotels are distributed over three storeys, with 250 rooms, distributed in an irregular manner, with garden terraces or roofs covered with volcanic soil, integrating the walls of the slopes into the same building. Adapting the design of these units to the topography ensures that all rooms have excellent views.

The resort also has three residential areas surrounding the hotel area. They all have individual accesses, despite being integrated into the landscape and the circulatory system of the complex. The communal areas are developed close to the beach and limited by the ravine: bars, a club, restaurants and an informal beach bar.

The aim of the project is to preserve the terrain and landscape of the area, bringing individuality to the complex and distancing itself from the majority of stereotypical resorts. The aim is to try to bring guests and residents closer to the beautiful natural setting that surrounds them. The project was developed by GCA Arquitectos Asociados and AE Land 1988 as the landscape architect.

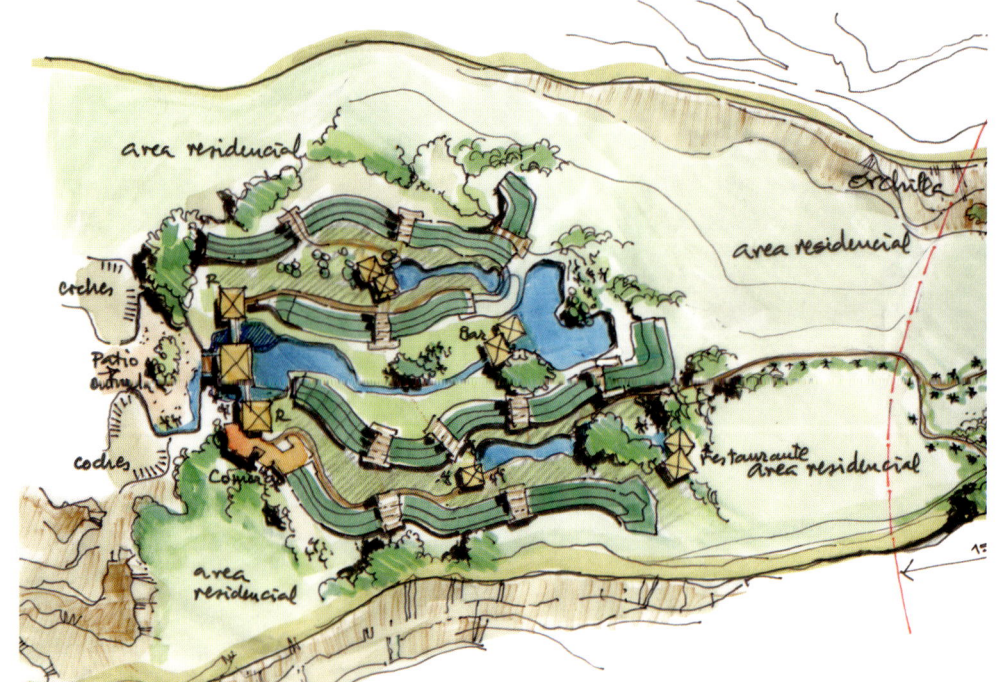

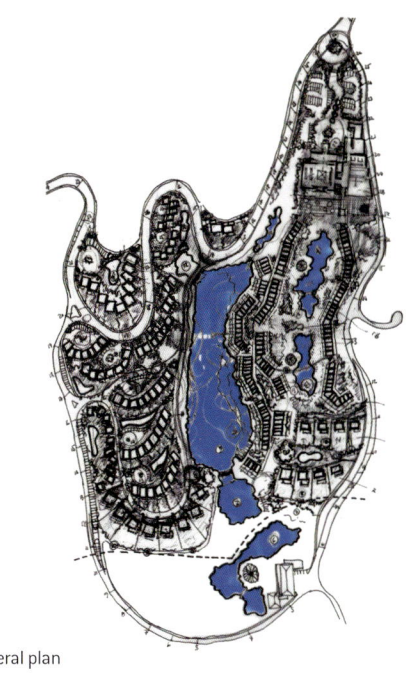

General plan

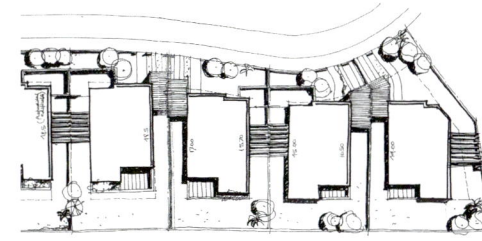

Section through apartments

Apartments plans

CONDOHOTEL MOJÁCAR FOR GROUP MED

Mojácar, Spain // 2006

General plan

The plan was to develop on a plot of 395,574 sq ft with 80% suitable for building, 77 fractional ownership units, 242 hotel condominium units, a Village with commercial areas, services (a fitness center, swimming pools and restaurants) and a parking lot.

The principle challenge consisted of adapting the volume to be built to the natural landscape morphology. The colors of the land, valleys, rocks, the protected plant of the area, the everlasting flower of Mojácar, and views of the golf course and sea are all outstanding features. The vegetation, incorporated into the architecture in earth-sheltered planted roofs, contrasts with white plaster and stone walls.

Circulation is structured around two access points and a main ring road. The private access is located in the western area of the lot, and public access in the east, a short walk from the site. The ring road provides access to each of the different sectors in the complex. The backbone of the complex is the Main Area, which includes the general reception area with the restrooms, meeting areas and the fitness/spa area, and ends with the Village. In order to adapt to the topography, the Village becomes the hub where the activities converge; they are organized in successive terraces from levels 37 to 15. Water is the main design element, and it generates different types of spaces or areas of interest at different levels, defining the identity of the three apartment group sectors.

The proposed differentiation of the sectors not only responds to topographic factors, but also to the possible phases of the project, so that each sector can function independently.

Roof plan of the central axis

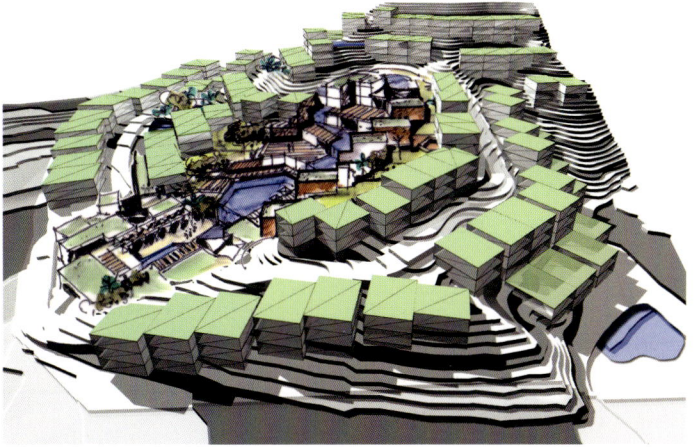

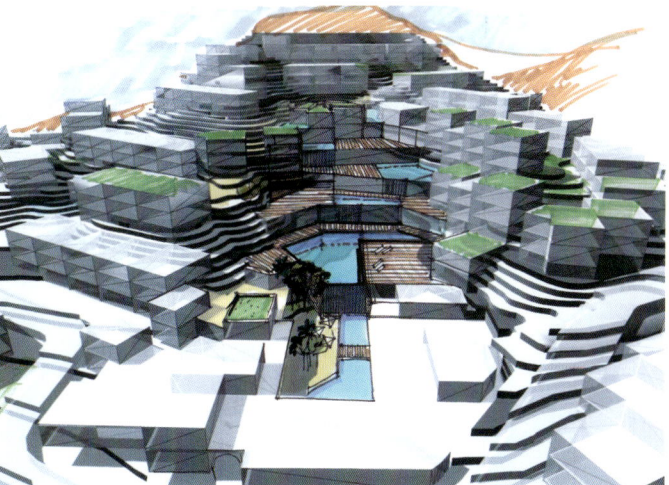

Sections　　　　　　　　　　　　　　　　General perspectives

CONDOHOTEL MOJÁCAR FOR GROUP MED // 187

SAN BASILIO HOTEL RESORT

Baja California, Mexico // 1997

General view of the *jameo* connecting the hall and the restaurant

Descent to the living area

Punta San Basilio is one of the most stunning enclaves in Baja California; it stands out for the virginal beauty of its land and beaches, which boast large undeveloped stretches of coastline. Access to the bay is through a valley. From its highest peak you can make out the San Basilio beach and the mountains. The 161,458 sq ft hotel complex was to be built on the hidden side of the mountain. After leaving the valley, a winding road ascends to an elevation of 50 above sea level. This is where you find the hotel's main entrance, a large esplanade with native vegetation, where you can watch the sunrise and sunset. In the middle of this plaza there is a large hole, like a jameo, where a grand staircase, which follows the curvature of the hole and frames an aquatic garden, leads to the lower floor. The social areas of the complex, including reception, hall, restaurant, bar and several lounges can be found on this level.

Below this area there are 100 junior apartment suites, forming successive terraces that are fully integrated into the topography, with earth-sheltered roofs, naturally insulating the rooms. This part of the building descends irregularly, following the contours of the terrain, reaching an oasis at the bottom of the valley. The 50 master suites are located on the opposite slope. Thus, both sides of this small colony extend across the slopes until they naturally join when they reach the oasis, the river that runs through the valley.

The second social area is located in this small natural oasis, with a bar, restaurant and pool, also with spectacular views of Manglito Bay, the rock wharf and the islets of Santa Estela and Nido.

View of the site

Interior view of the living area

Access view

Model images

Perspective of the bungalows in the beach area

190 // HOTELS

THERAPEUTIC-TOURISM COMPLEX

Sanillés, Spain // 1994

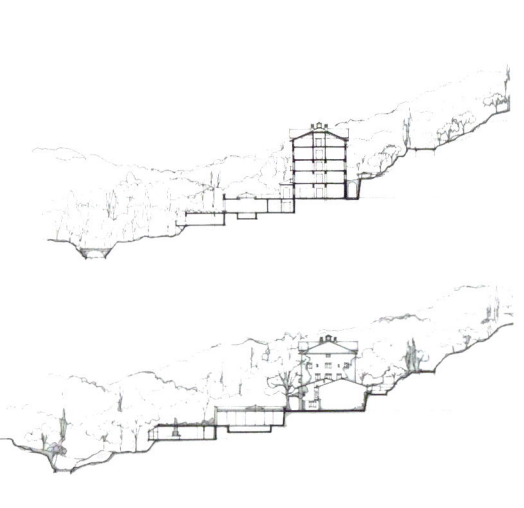

Cross section

The idea of designing this therapeutic-tourism community came from the Institut Terapèutic Internacional de Catalunya. Its aim is to improve the welfare of people with different illnesses or disabilities, who often are confined to their own homes due to the lack of facilities provided with disabled access.

The location of the project in the Catalan Pyrenees provided a healthy setting, away from pollution and the bustle of urban areas. This is a space that invites relaxation in close contact with nature. It has been planned to remove the architectural barriers that may obstruct the mobility of residents in the complex. The project involved the restoration of the existing hotel and the development of the resort, which has three sectors. The first one is located under the terrace of the old building, where the spa area for rehabilitation therapies is located. The studios for blind and mobility-impaired people are located below this space.

The second sector houses two and three bedroom homes, with no architectural barriers, using the terraces of the existing site as a base on which the project was planned. Finally, the third and final area at the end of the valley contains three and four bedroom homes, designed for people with disabilities who wish to live with their families in a suitable environment, designed especially for them.

Project perspectives

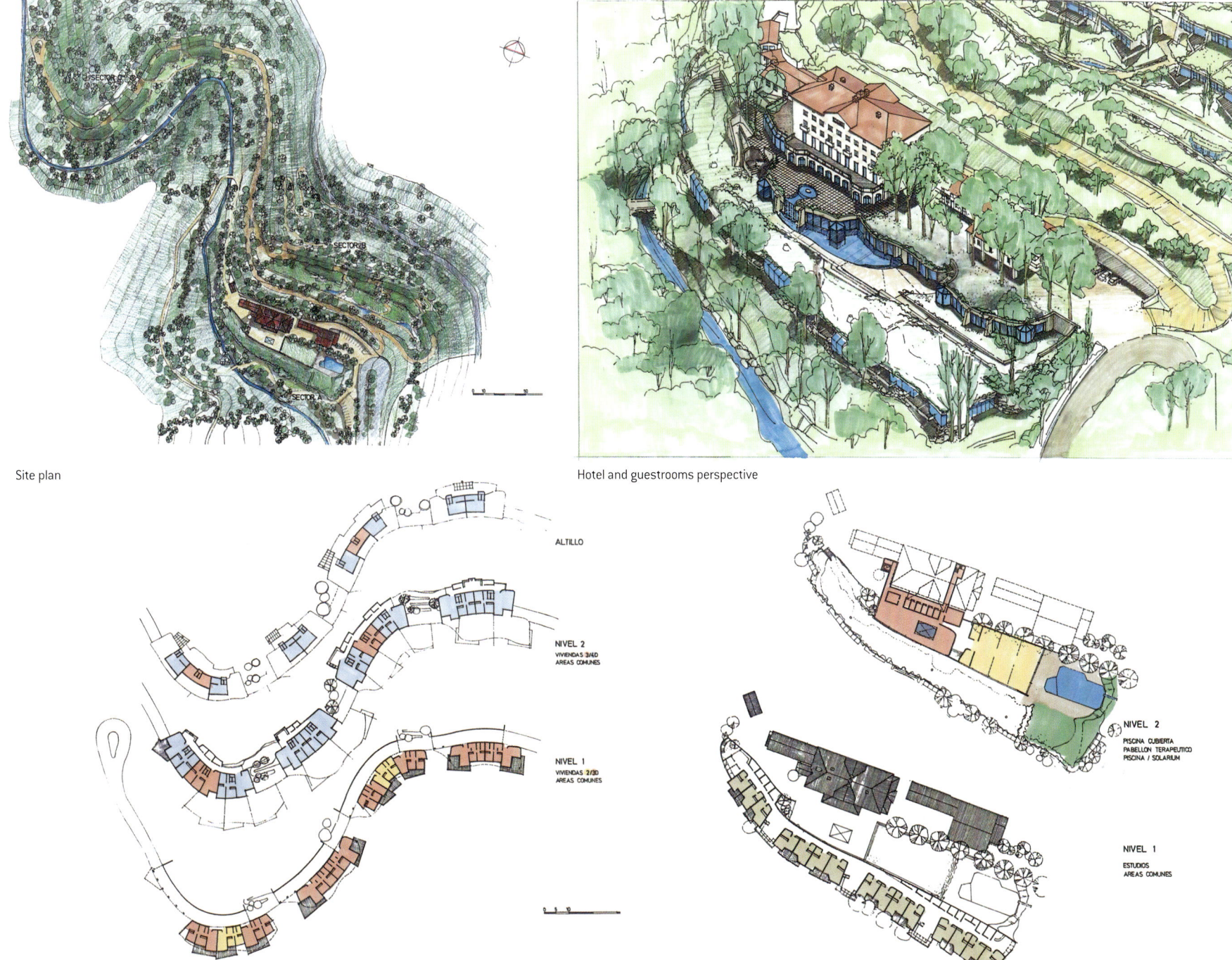

Site plan

Hotel and guestrooms perspective

Guestrooms disposition

Hotel zone

OUED BOUTIQUE HOTEL ©

Marrakech, Morocco // 2010

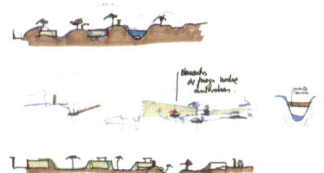

Section sketches of the site

Site view

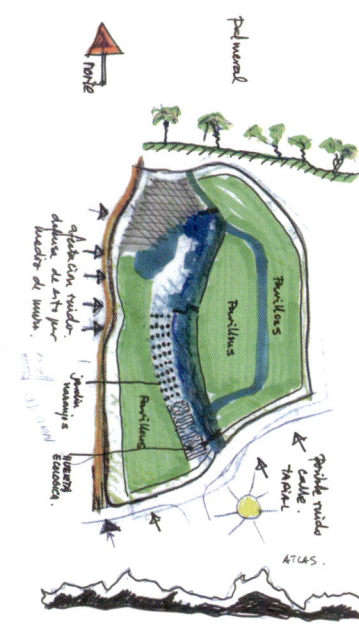

Site study

General view

Cross section

Water is the essence of this project, born from the idea of creating an artificial river from an existing topographic feature in the terrain. The river becomes the backbone of the hotel, and water is the creative element both for the landscape and the urban design. The idea of water and garden as inseparable elements is reflected in the food-producing gardens: with fruit trees, vegetables and seasonal herbs that are used in the hotel's kitchen.

This "boutique hotel" is built on a site of 16 acres and consists of a main building and three types of bungalows in individual lots, with a total built area of 88,264 sq ft.

Circulation is solved with an outer route for electric vehicles and secondary paths that give access to the bungalows, through a hierarchy of public spaces formed by plazas and gardens. Pedestrian routes are treated with special care, offering guests a variety of pathways and bridges that link the different areas on both sides of the artificial river.

The main volume of the three-storey hotel is the arrival and assembly point. On the first floor, the lobby, administration, several lounges, a bar and two restaurants are located while the top floor is exclusively dedicated to suites. The parking lot and general services area are located in the basement, and the spa is located in a terraced area by the river that runs through the whole complex. The design of the gardens and the river is completed with three types of bungalows: "presidential", with a unique design that seeks maximum privacy and best views of the river and the Atlas, "senior" in the highest part of the lot and built on terraces at various levels, in a Moroccan casbah-style, and finally "junior", that are surrounded by spaces with the essence of the traditional Islamic plazas and gardens.

GREEN UNDER GREEN

Barcelona, Spain // 1986

The competition for the design of this sports and entertainment complex in the district of Sant Gervasi was organized by Barcelona City Council. The winning proposal was carried out along with the architectural firm L35. The complex, which at that time was the largest underground sports center in Europe, covering a total of 376,736 sq ft, was constructed beneath the surface of the park and outdoor pools. These pools, with a transparent floor at different points, illuminate the halls of this huge underground complex consisting of several gyms and fitness rooms, paddle and squash courts and additional services. A parking lot consisting of three levels with a total of 1,000 spaces was constructed under these installations.

At ground level a 21,527 sq ft farmhouse-style building was restored, located on the corner, for catering services and hosting events. The project also included burying the circular-plan Sant Gregory Thaumaturgus church, located on the square going by the same name, under a large fountain with a glass bottom through which light would penetrate.

Due to the scale of the intervention, the provision of sports equipment and services and, crucially, owing to the concept of burying the building and to salvage a large park in the area, the project represented a milestone in a consolidated urban sector and is unique in Barcelona. Its success lies in integrating the project into the city and on the intensive use, not only by local people, but also by a large number of people working in the area who can enjoy the wide range of sporting activities, in addition to outdoor recreational areas, movie theaters and a wide variety of local restaurants.

Views of finished project

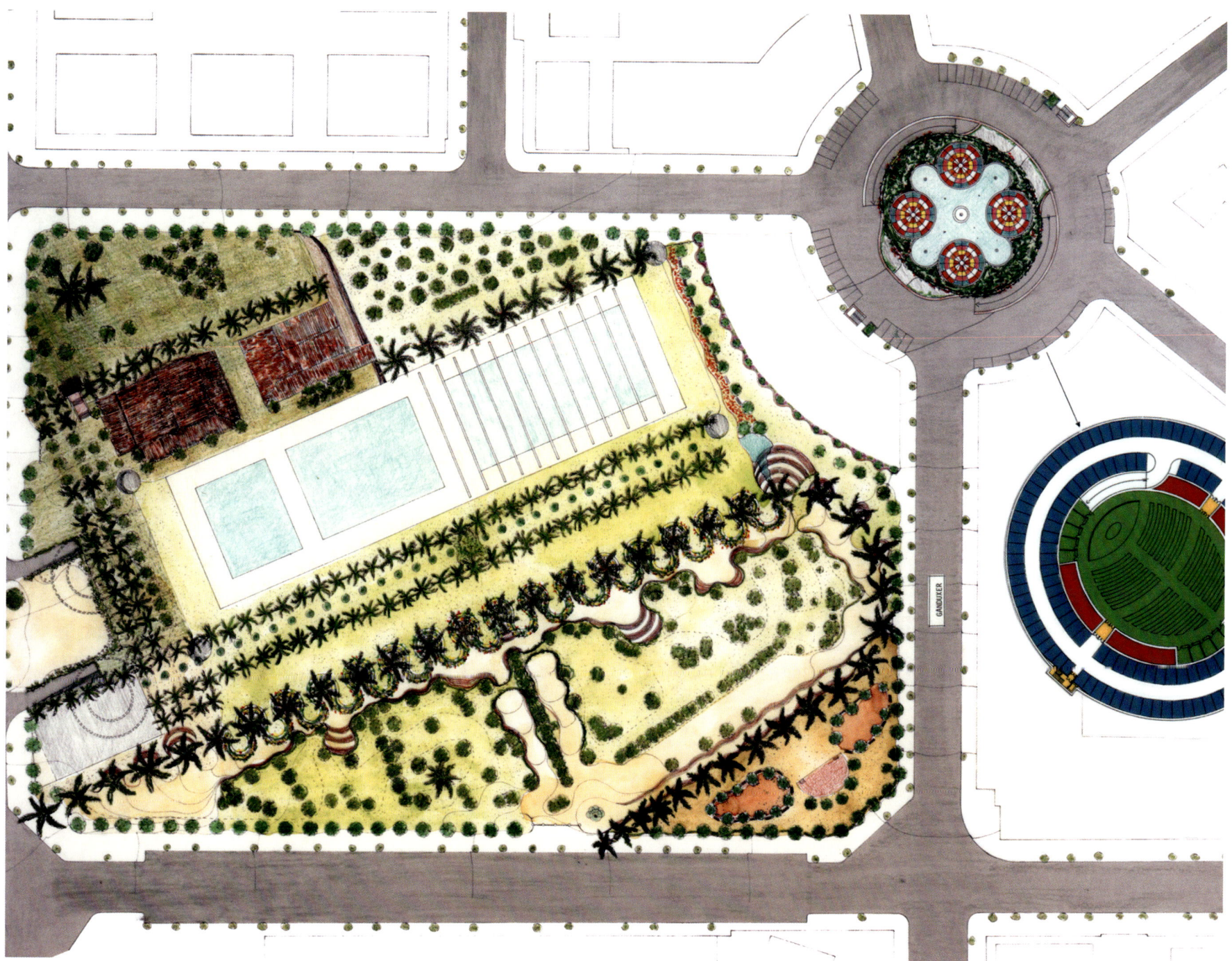

General plan

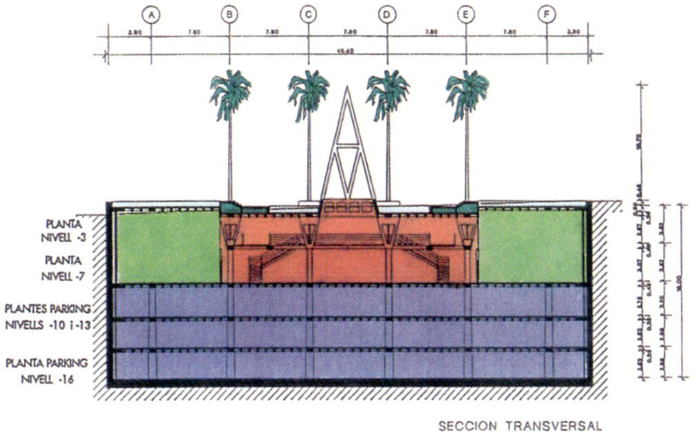
PLANTA
NIVELL -3
PLANTA
NIVELL -7
PLANTES PARKING
NIVELLS -10 i -13
PLANTA PARKING
NIVELL -16
SECCION TRANSVERSAL

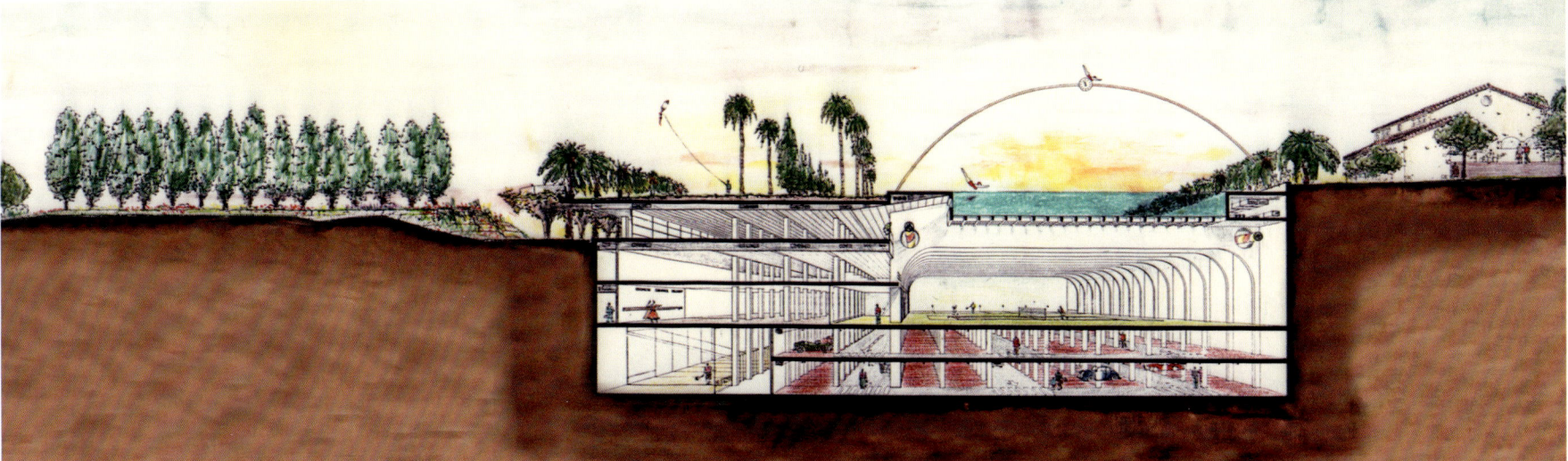

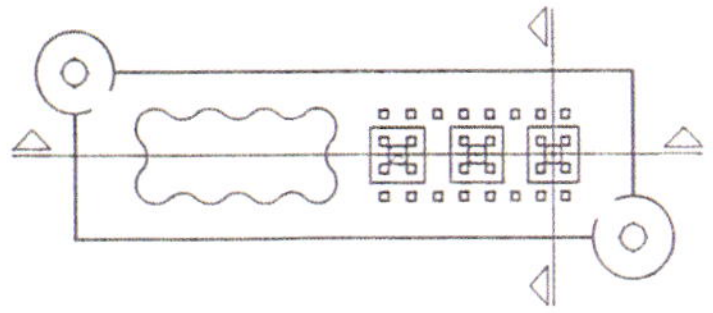

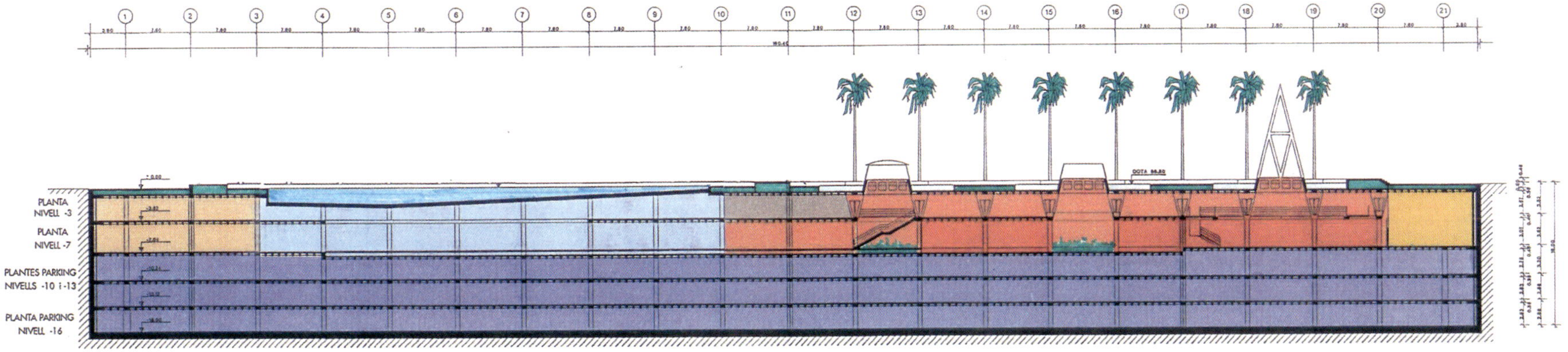
PLANTA
NIVELL -3
PLANTA
NIVELL -7
PLANTES PARKING
NIVELLS -10 i -13
PLANTA PARKING
NIVELL -16

Sections

RCD ESPANYOL SHOPPING MALL

Cornellà de Llobregat, Spain // 2002

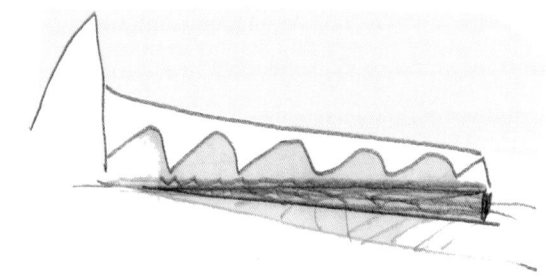

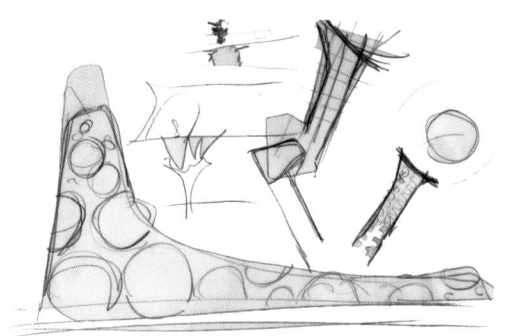

This project was submitted to a competition for a complex for commercial (269,097 sq ft) and leisure (322,917 sq ft) use on the triangular site adjacent to the lot where the RCD Espanyol soccer field would be constructed.

Members of the team working on the project commissioned by Amstelland MDC nv included the companies FCC Construcción S. A., and Proinosa.

The essence of the Estudio BC's proposal lies in the two wings that form the building. One of wings is permeable and open to the existing park and to the city. The other, however, seeks to protect the complex from the fast traffic on the Cinturón Litoral acting as a large acoustic screen. The two wings are linked through a series of volumes that form a plaza-park in the center. The different architectural treatment of the façades reinforces the various functions of each volume.

The building sector nearest to the city is placed under an accessible roof garden connecting the different commercial floors across a gentle incline. It acts as an extension of the park, turning this access to the mall into an attractive scenic route. This building-park is erected on a oxidized concrete façade facing the street, with large arches that emerge from the ground while giving a glimpse of the stores inside. The other wing of the building that contains the entertainment sector, is surrounded by a pierced COR-TEN wall-screen that protects the complex from the noise of the traffic while serving as an advertising space.

In between the two wings, a series of glass volumes lead down to the plaza surrounded by green patios, accessible terraces and ponds.

A recessed patio-garden is the exit from the lower levels, connecting the two levels of parking lots and leading to the Plaza shopping mall and the soccer field.

Initial façade ideas

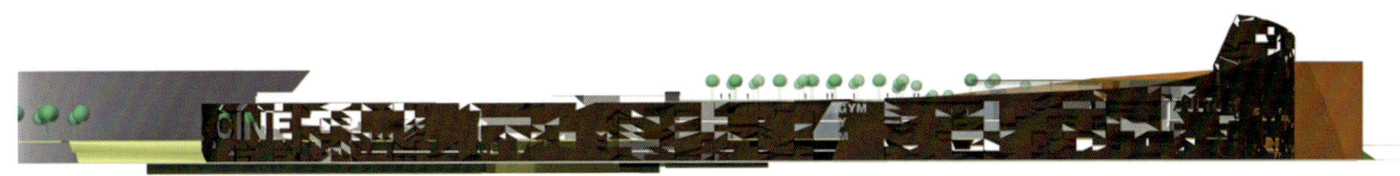

Elevations

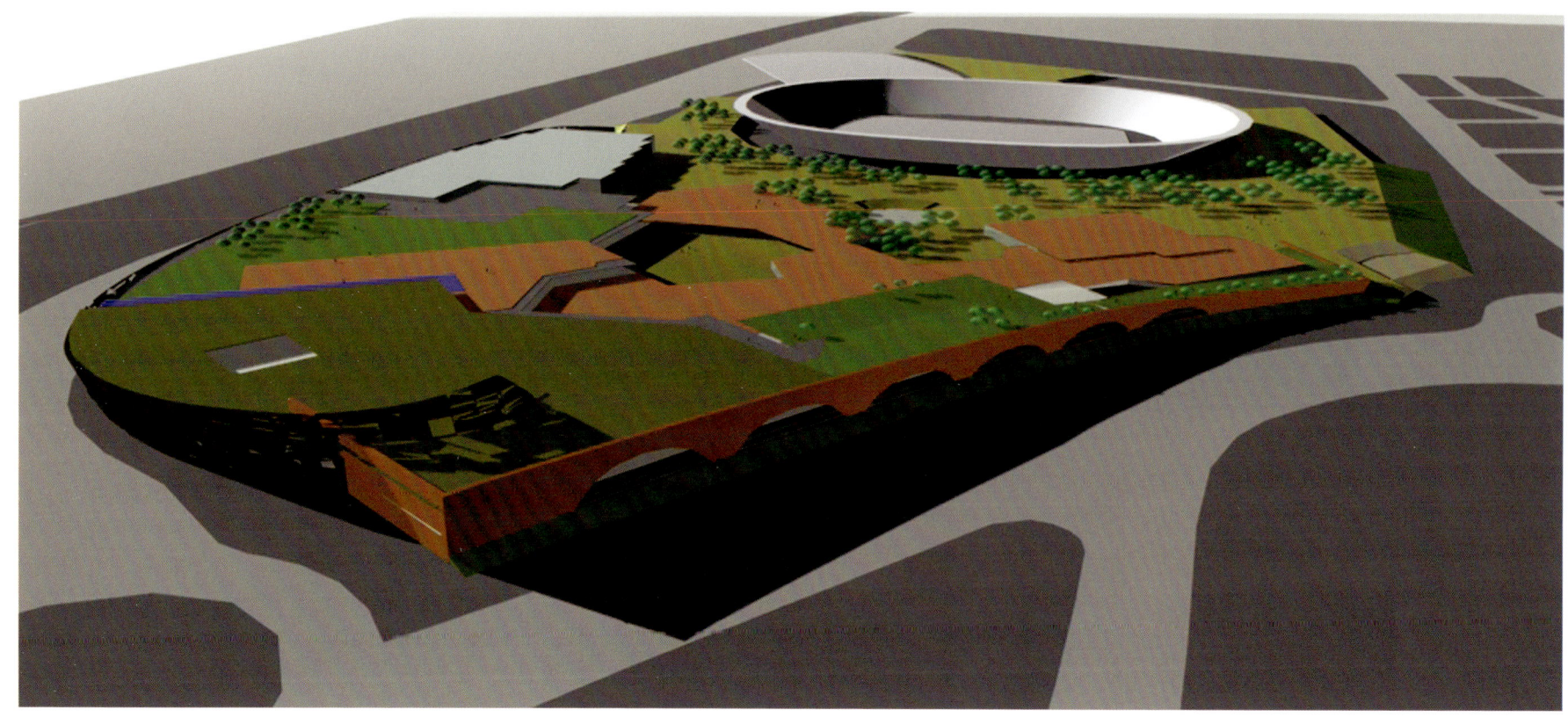
General view

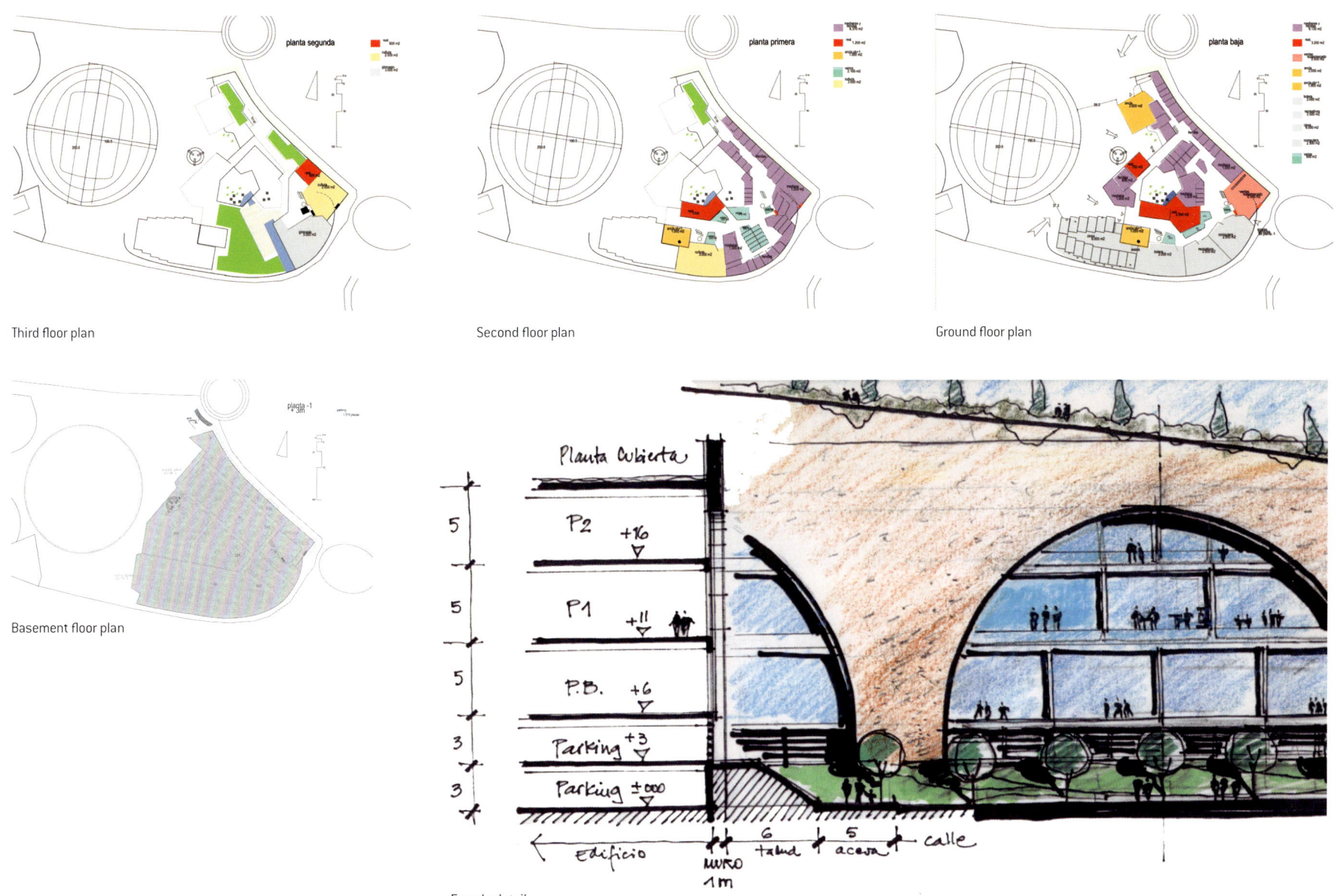

Third floor plan

Second floor plan

Ground floor plan

Basement floor plan

Façade detail

RCD ESPANYOL SHOPPING MALL // 203

ALICE IN WONDERLAND. KRISTIANSAND PERFORMING ARTS CENTER

Kristiansand, Norway // 2005

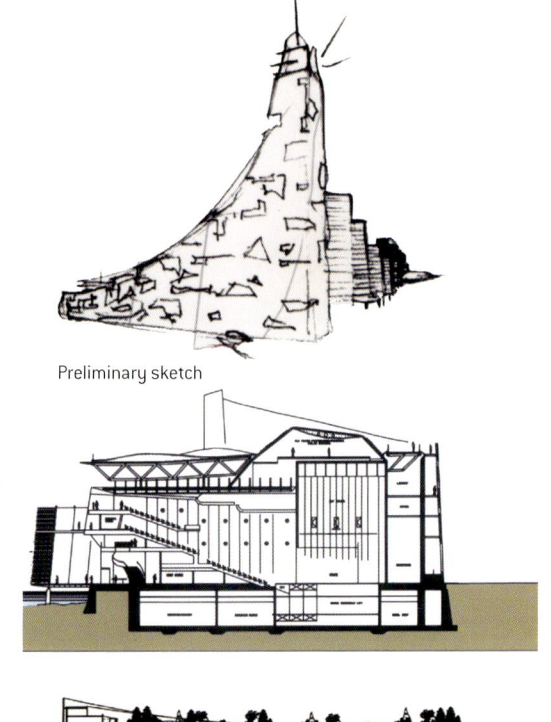

Preliminary sketch

The proposal for this project was made by Javier Barba's studio for the architectural competition for a scenic arts and entertainment center in the Norwegian city of Kristiansand in 2005. In the design and development of the project Estudio BC worked with the American architect Illya Azaroff, secretary of the AIA. Although their work was carried out in their respective cities (Azaroff and his team in New York and the Estudio BC, in Barcelona), the two are united by the passion for architecture.

The complex, located on a former industrial site, had to include different spaces: a theater, concert hall, a theater studio, rehearsal rooms, restaurants, educational facilities and administration offices. The proposal, which was named as the favorite by the citizens in the local press, was conceived as a 'green' building. The ventilated façade is composed of three layers, one of COR-TEN steel and two of glass, among which visitors can stroll, and which offers good thermal performance in the interior of the building. Translucent towers also act as thermal regulators. The COR-TEN of the façade is a tribute to the memories of the old iron ships stranded in the ports.

The complex is designed as a continuation of the natural terrain where the water meets the trees and the green roof. As sustainable measures, the building incorporates water treatment for reuse and three geothermal wells. A central plaza is located both inside and outside the building, allowing visitors to enjoy views from the viewpoints and balconies of the complex.

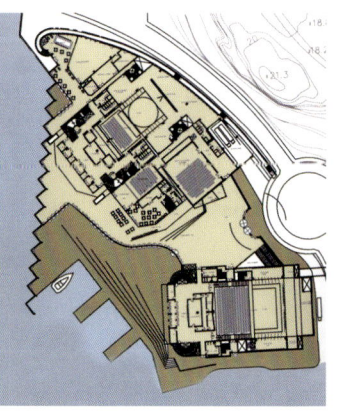

General plans

CLUB HOUSE. GOLF LA GRAIERA

Calafell, Spain // 2009

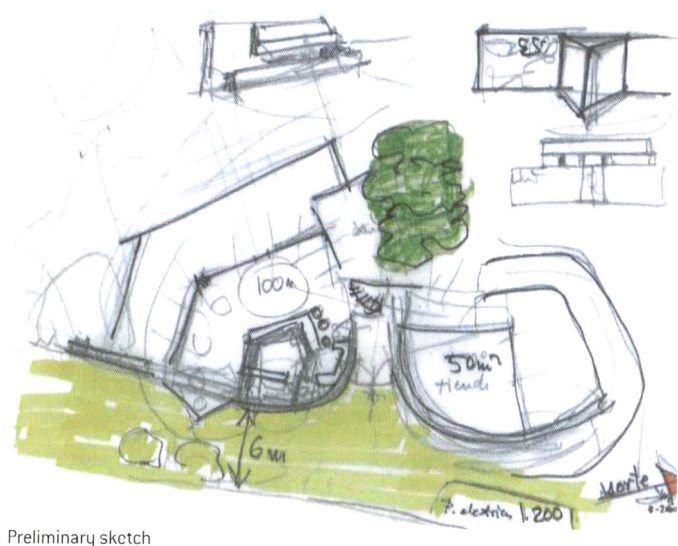

Preliminary sketch

The project is based on the construction of the club house for La Graiera golf club, an 18-hole golf course and a pitch & putt course in a bow-shaped lot with an east-west facing slope. The building is situated on the widest part of the site and its design achieves the best views and orientation.

Two impressive curved walls form the basic structure of the architectural volume. These meet in the entrance of the building forming the hall and are organized around the cylindrical volume of the staircase. They also enclose and arrange the various program activities on three levels on both sides of the hall: the first floor houses the social spaces, bar, restaurant, lounge, shop and offices; the basement houses the dressing rooms, storage and a garage for golf carts, and finally, the roof for use in summer, with a chill out candle-lit terrace-bar. The tower that houses the staircase provides the building with a unique feature.

The use of stone, concrete, corten steel and wood establishes a relationship between the material, color and the setting. The garden extends from the outdoor terraces on the first floor level, with the lounge areas. Plant species that need little water and the incorporation of a traditional dry stone shepherd's hut that already existed on the site contribute to the garden. The program comes complete with two parking lots: one to the back of the building, with one reserved for loading and unloading, and another across the cobblestone street and green spaces that provides access to the clubhouse. Other ring roads and paths were designed connecting the area with the different areas of the golf course.

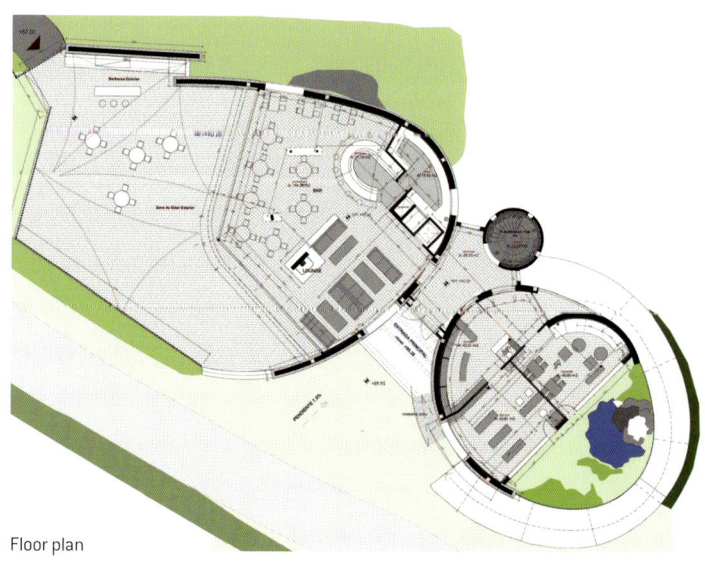

Floor plan

CLUB HOUSE. GOLF LA GRAIERA

West elevation

North elevation

East elevation

South elevation

Images of the work in progress

CLUB HOUSE AND SPA IN POLAND

Warsaw, Poland // 2009

Preliminary sketch

This project, a few miles from Warsaw, was awarded first prize in the international competition organized by the owner. The three areas of the club are arranged around a curved axis: a porch-series of arches, forming a large square with different levels, with a paved surface with green areas. The clubhouse and convention center on level 102 and the spa and meditation center on level 98 can be accessed from the esplanade. In between these buildings there is a green area with a garden and pool overlooking the golf course.

The club house is composed of three levels. The lower level houses the service areas, changing rooms and storage for golf carts. The first floor is home to the main entrance, reception, administration, living rooms, bar, restaurants and shops. Its distribution guarantees the best views and includes terraces facing holes 9 and 18 and the tee 1. The second floor, on level 106 is reserved for VIP members.

The convention center is connected to the club house through a hall which means that common areas and restrooms can be shared. The porch, a continuous axis linking the entrances to the building, turns into a wooden and glass bridge that reaches the spa and meditation center. These areas incorporate feng shui concepts with different areas depending on use. The lower level, facing south, houses the spa area with treatment rooms, arranged in a circular form: sun-life-heat-fire-touch. Café Manipura, located in the center, attached to the land, represents stability, support and home. The water area facing north-south conveys flexibility and on the higher level facing east-west is the meditation room, a space for reflection.

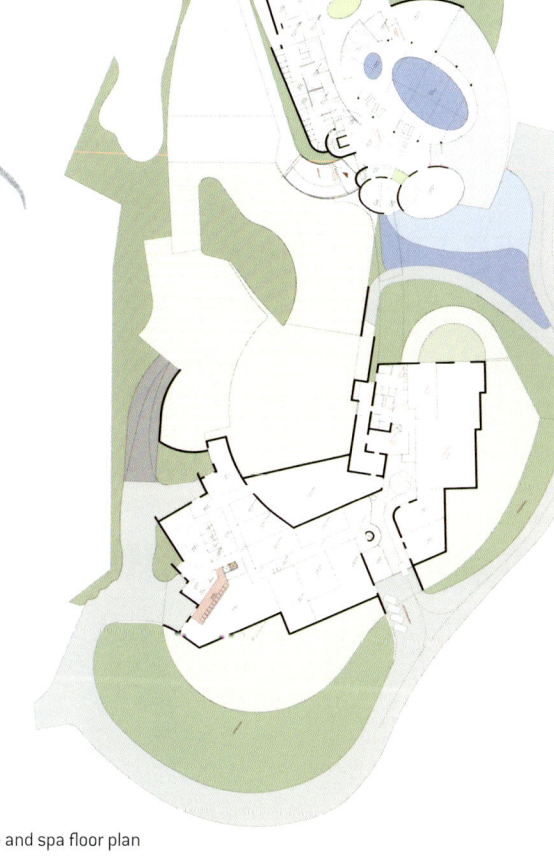
Club and spa floor plan

General section

General plan

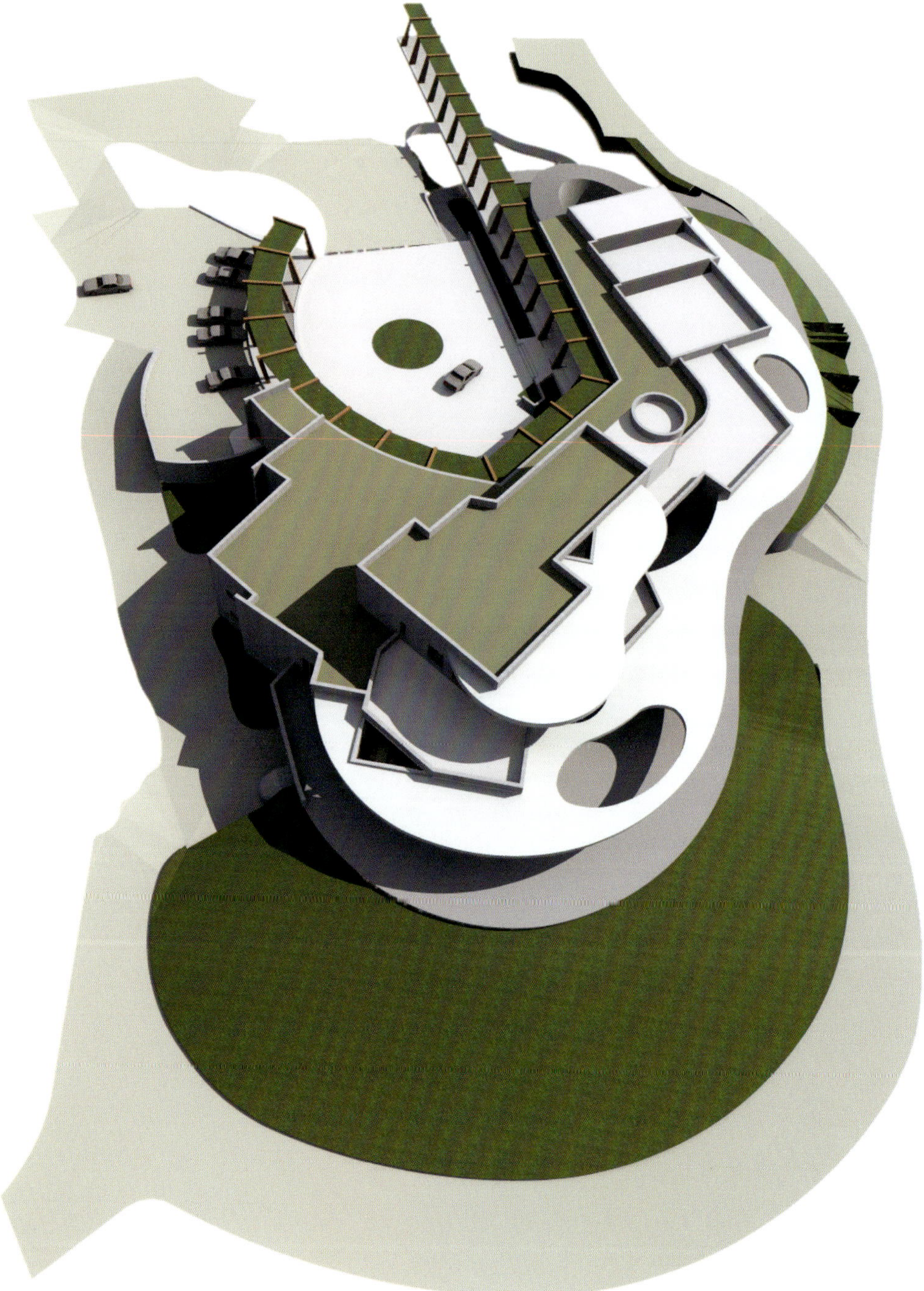

View of the club

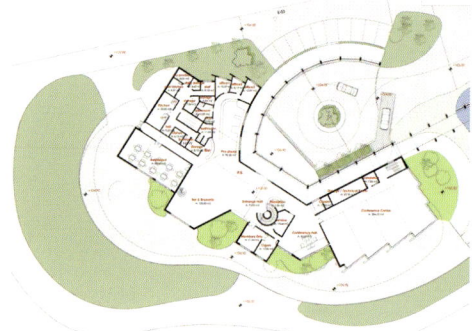

Club floor plan

Spa floor plan

212 // SPORTS AND LEISURE FACILITIES

Version 1

Version 2

CLUB HOUSE AND SPA IN POLAND // 213

STAG'S LEAP WINE CELLARS

Napa Valley, California, USA // 1999

Tradition and the extraordinary quality of wine produced by this family wine cellar must be reflected in a unique architectural complex. The client became extremely involved with the architect in developing the proposal. This collaboration forged a firm friendship between Warren Winiarski, his son Stephen and Javier Barba, and the result was a balanced and impressive project among the large trees and existing rocks.

One objective was to define the finishes of the two areas that can be found in the underground path: the Round Room, crowned with a large vault and located in the intersection of several tunnels and the Great Room, where special guests are received. The wine cellar also has five entrances or different doorways. The project was to present a solution for each of them, but with a common architectural idea that would link them.

The Estudio BC proposal that reflects all these interventions was The Arcade, a porch-series of arches that connects, communicates and enables visitors to be under shelter throughout the entire route. The design unifies and frames the two access doors to the wine cellar, leading to the Great Room, the library and the area adjacent to the kitchen for events. Behind these rooms a labyrinth of tunnels can be accessed, the junction of which is the Round Room, where a Foucault pendulum recalls the passage of time. The irregular-shaped paving is made from natural quartzite tiles, the shotcrete walls are mixed with mica to create reflections simulating the sky and the lighting was resolved with lights on the ground and with the design of perforated copper cones on the walls. The doorways were designed with motifs that combine iron or wood with glass. The completion of this project led to the realization of a second project – the visitor center and tasting room – in 2003.

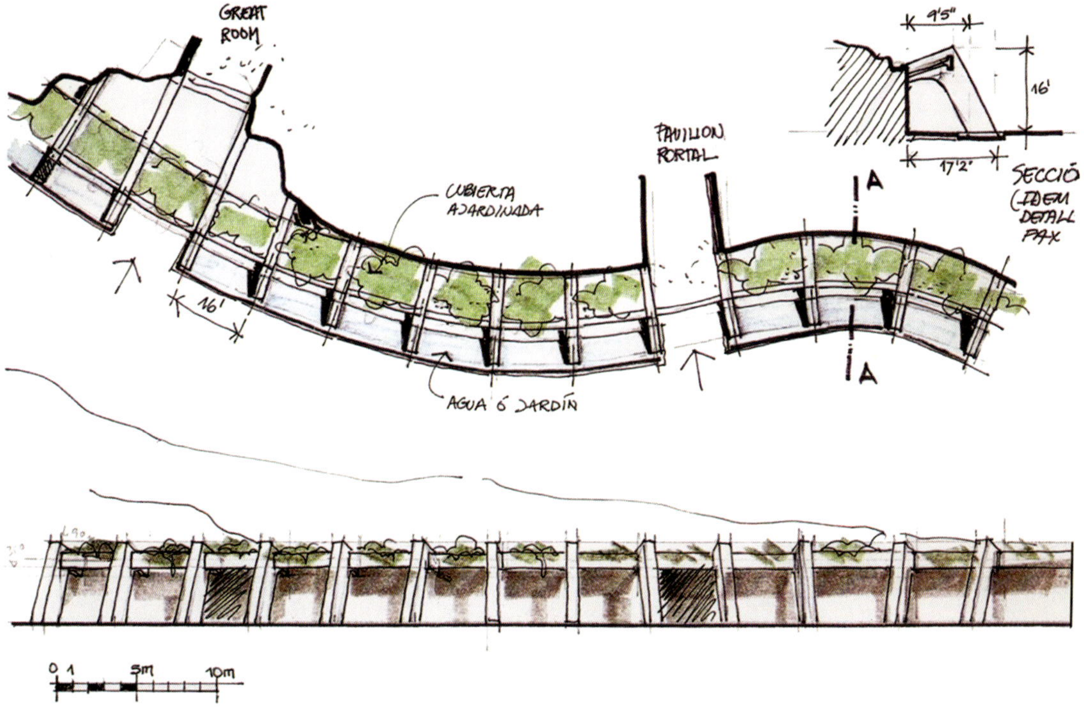

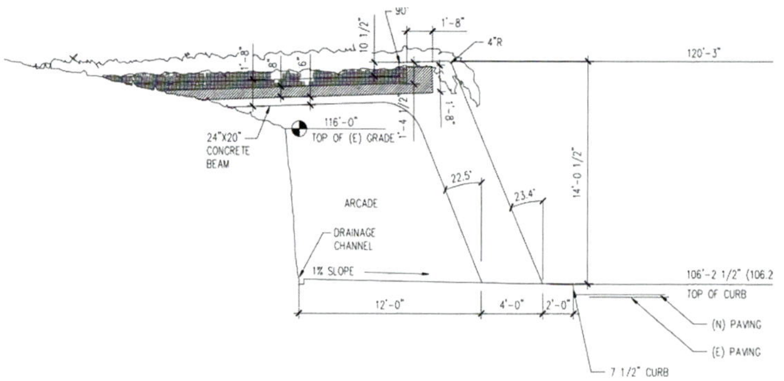

Arcade details

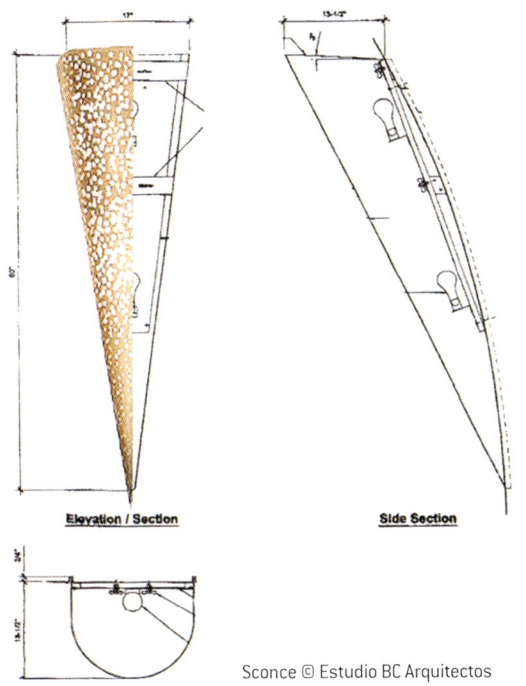

Sconce © Estudio BC Arquitectos

STAG'S LEAP WINE CELLARS // 219

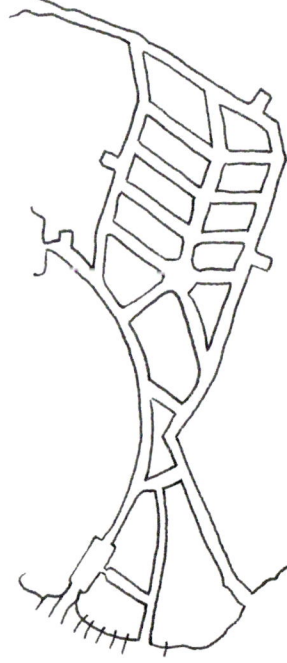

Scheme of the underground tunnels

STAG'S LEAP WINE CELLARS VISITOR CENTER

Napa Valley, California, USA // 2003

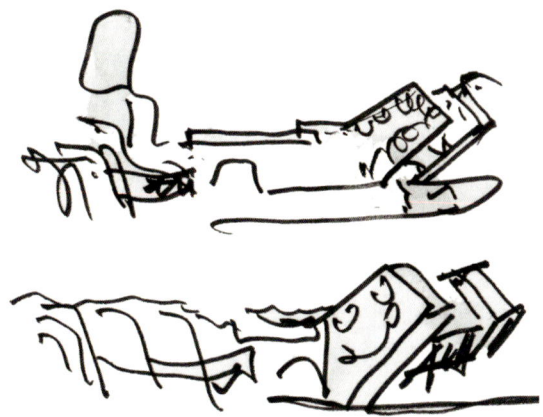

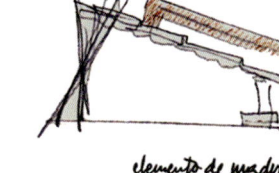
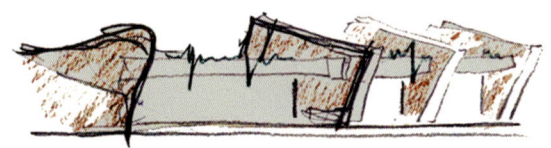

Sketch evolution

The visitor center is the second phase of a project that Estudio BC began with the construction of the winery. The new building, with a series of spaces that bring the world of wine closer to visitors, is erected in a plaza, from which the vineyards and the rest of the estate can be viewed.

From the lobby you can access the private and group tasting rooms. The latter has two bars, one with its back to the landscape, allowing visitors to taste the wine with the exciting backdrop of the vast vineyards and the mountains. This feeling of spaciousness is enhanced in architectural terms by the actual amount of space, defined by thick stone walls. The flat wooden roof covers half of the room, and then it slants upward meeting the vast windows that extend from the roof and descend to the ground in the northern part.

The volume is divided by four sturdy dark stone walls. Making use of the existing terraces, an outdoor terrace was designed for barbecues and tasting, with the same flooring as that used indoors in order to integrate the different areas. Part of the building houses the service areas for the organization of events. These are located at the rear, and their opaque façade contrasts with the front glass expanse. In order to unify the center, the same design guidelines were used to harmonize the building constructed in the first phase.

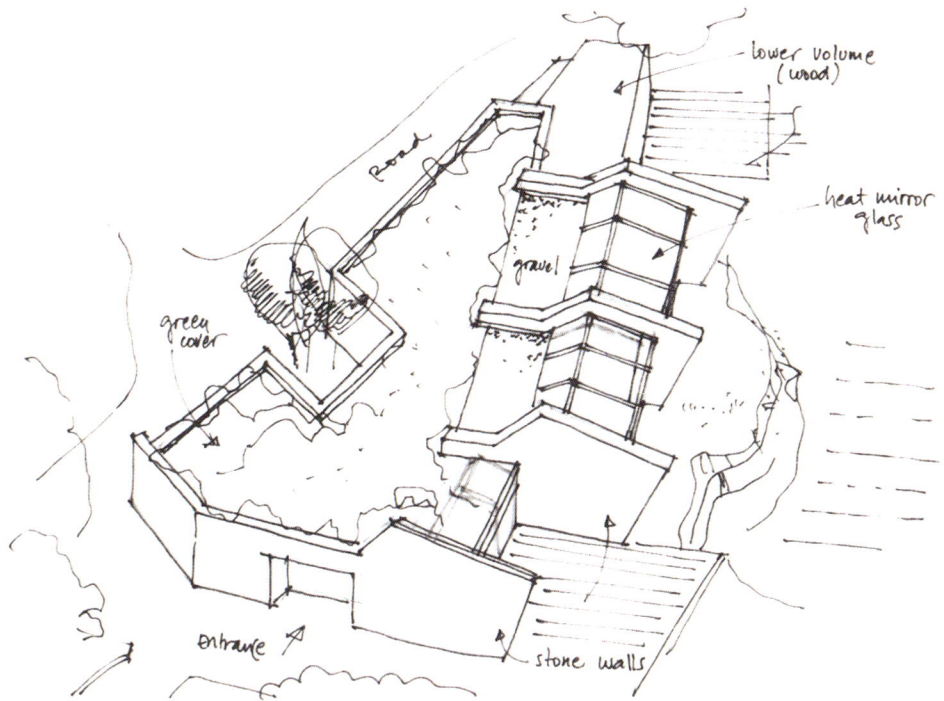

Axonometric

Tasting room

STAG'S LEAP WINE CELLARS VISITOR CENTER // 223

INTERVENTION IN SOTO DE TORRES FOR BODEGAS TORRES

La Rioja, Spain // 2009

The Bodegas Torres facilities in the Rioja Alavesa represents the introduction of this winery into a long-established Spanish wine region. The project had to convey the brand's philosophy: the introduction of sustainable factors, protection of the environment and integration into the environment. The existing building came into conflict with the environment owing to its dominant volume and the absence of organic lines. Given the location of the bodega on a hill, the building is visible from the surroundings, creating a visual impact.

The Estudio BC project had to tackle the issues of sustainability and adaptation to the environment. The project sought to integrate the existing volume into the surrounding environment. Finally, the proposal was completed with the development of the other buildings.

To merge the building into the landscape, colors and shapes were imitated. The natural breaks that make up the terraced vineyards inspire the perfect texture for the new façade of the bodega, bringing the landscape closer to the volume. Three concepts define this operation: concealment by the earth works, the disintegration, which seeks to integrate the building into the landscape through a skin or specific façade, using horizontality, transparency, or mimesis resources, and, finally, alignment, which alternates the building with the outlines of the landscape by breaking the current form. Shotcrete concrete mixed with local clayey soils was used for the finishing of the wall, providing plasticity and color to the building fulfilling the established objectives.

The project includes careful landscaping to recreate the local oak tree vegetation and trees were planted at points where they help to hide and integrate the façades of the buildings.

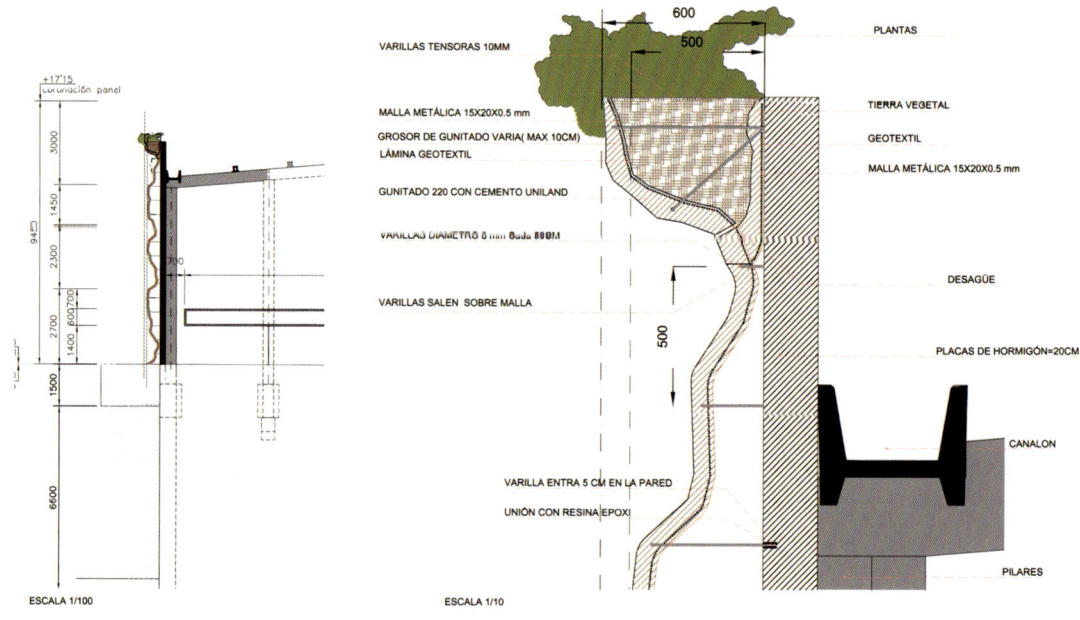

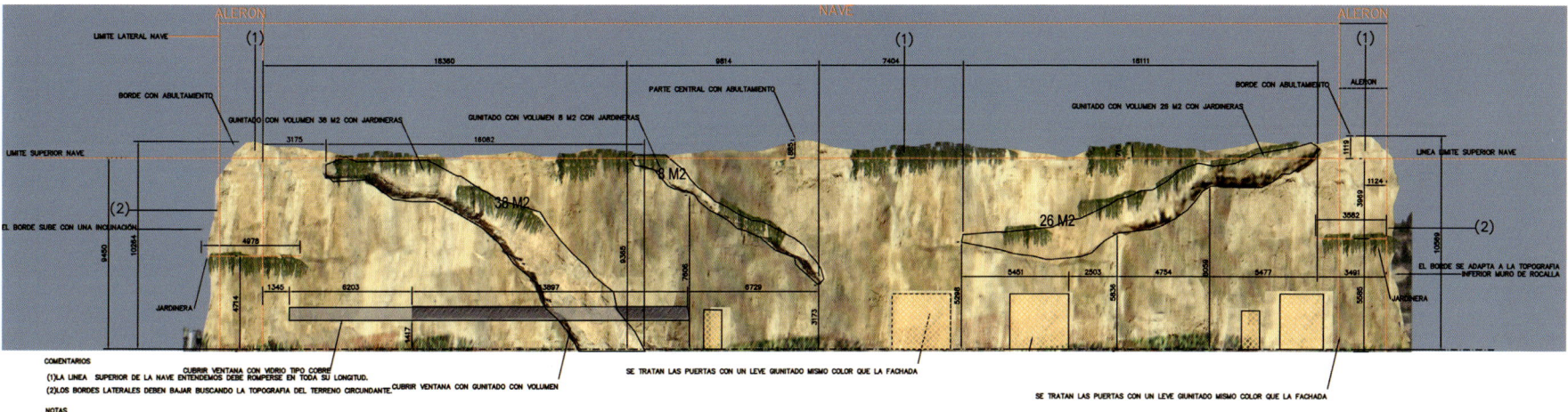

INTERVENTION IN SOTO DE TORRES FOR BODEGAS TORRES // 225

WALTRAUD CELLAR FOR BODEGAS TORRES

Vilafranca del Penedès, Spain // 2008

The Torres family requested Barba to create a place to present the best wines of their vineyard. From the outset it was clear that besides the technical aspects, the program should display the spirit and emotion of the wine, without falling into a theatrical design.

The project is divided into three levels, respecting the natural elevation of the land. The first underground level is where the barrels of wine are held in reserve. The second is developed as a cloister. This is a space for meditation and reflection that includes a fountain in the center representing an element of life and the flow of time. The transparent glass bottom of the fountain connects the center of the courtyard with the center of the underground plaza with a beam of light, symbolizing the union between the interior and exterior of the land. Finally, the third level houses a tasting room and museum. The simple and forceful forms of the volume are surrounded by water and are linked to the atrium by a waterfall.

The materials include COR-TEN steel and concrete, which is used in the large frieze of the arched square and chipped in the columns. Respect for the land is evident in the large earth-sheltered roof planted with local species to minimize water consumption. The installation of a photovoltaic tree creates the energy required to light up the complex.

The artistic collaboration includes sculptured pieces, such as the *Familia Reserva Pétre*a, by Xavier Corberó, guarding the entrance to the cloister, and *Mutus Liber*, by Josep Cerdà i Ferrer, in the reflecting pool in front of the tasting room. The tasting room features paintings by the artist Waltraud Maczassek.

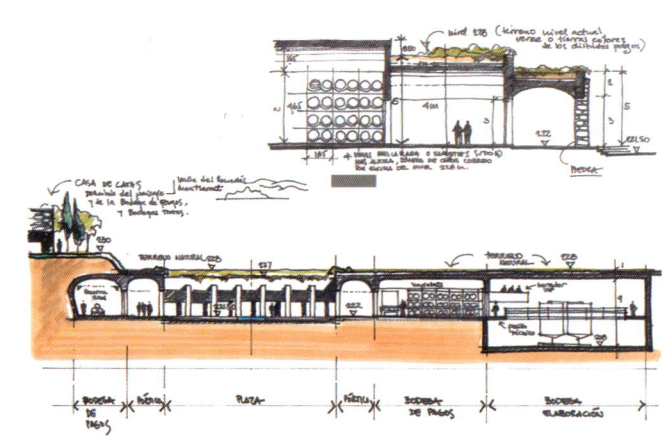
Preliminary sections

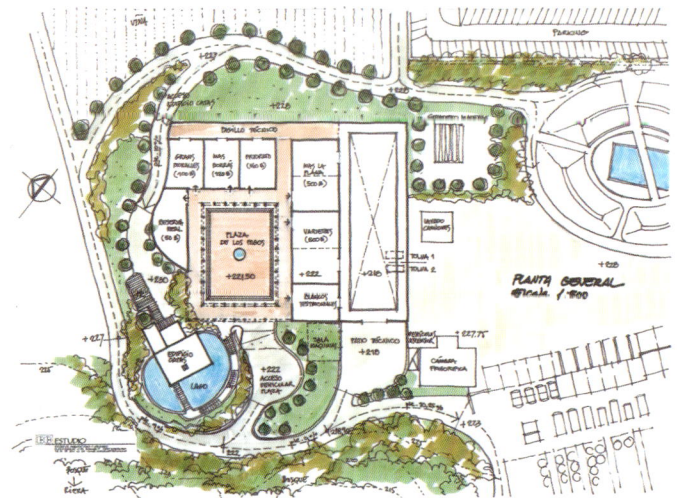
Floor plan

WALTRAUD CELLAR FOR BODEGAS TORRES

HRH PRINCE SULTAN BIN FAHAD RESIDENCE IN CANNES

Cannes, France // 2009

General plan

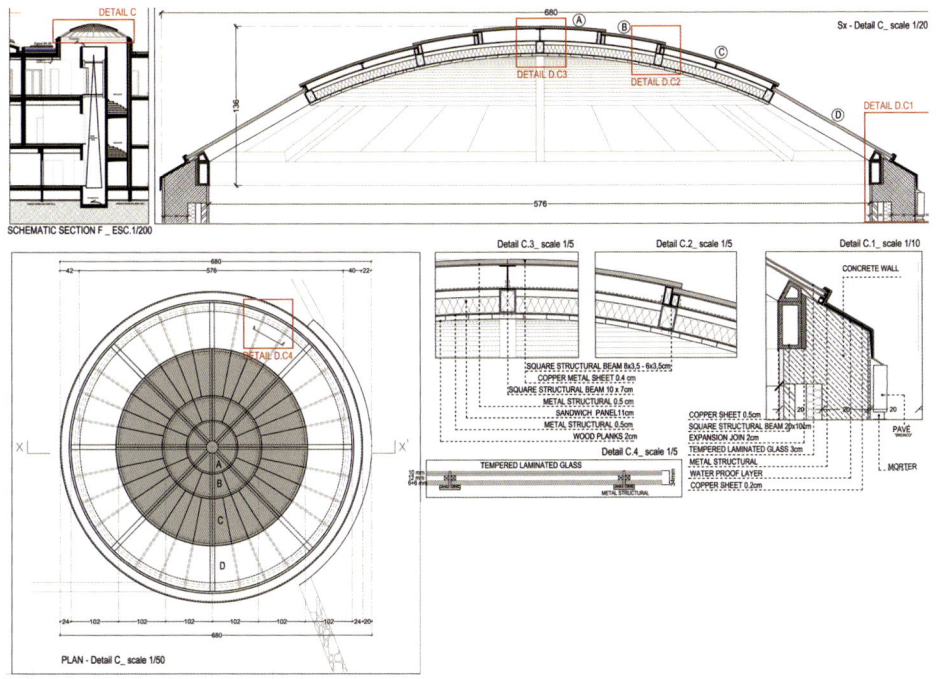

Detail of the skylight

OTHER PROJETS // 237

COLONQUES HOUSE

Minorca, Spain // 2003

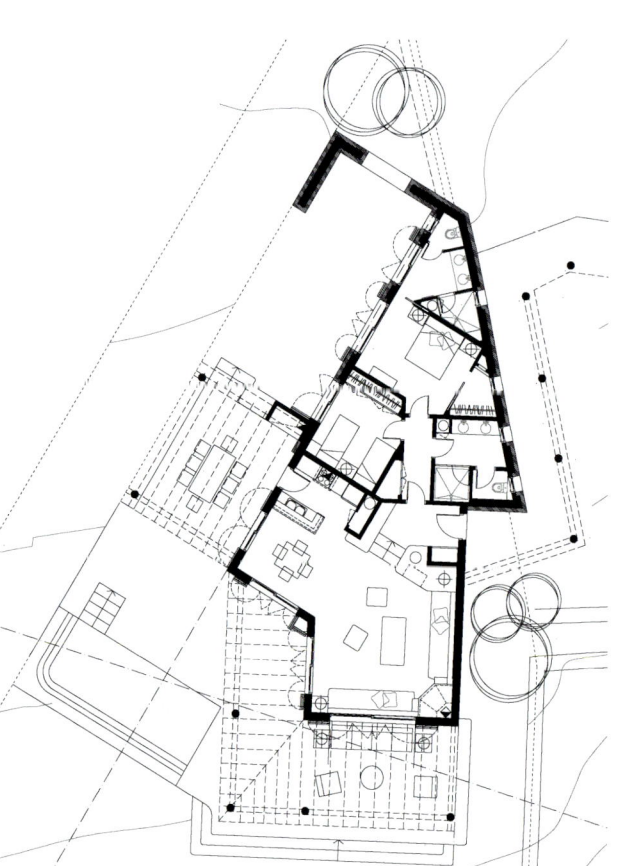

General plan

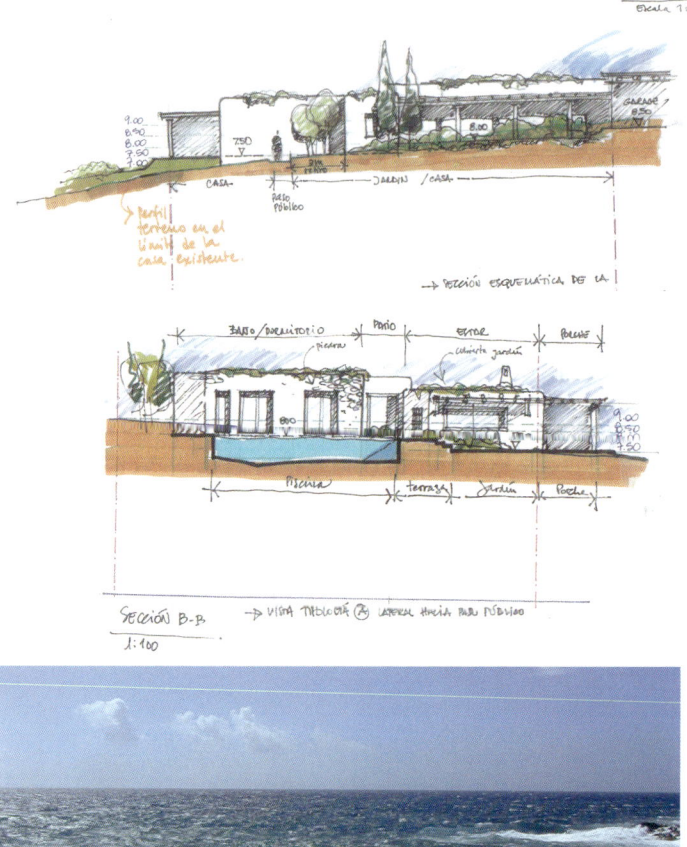

SWAROVSKI HOUSE

Minorca, Spain // 1999

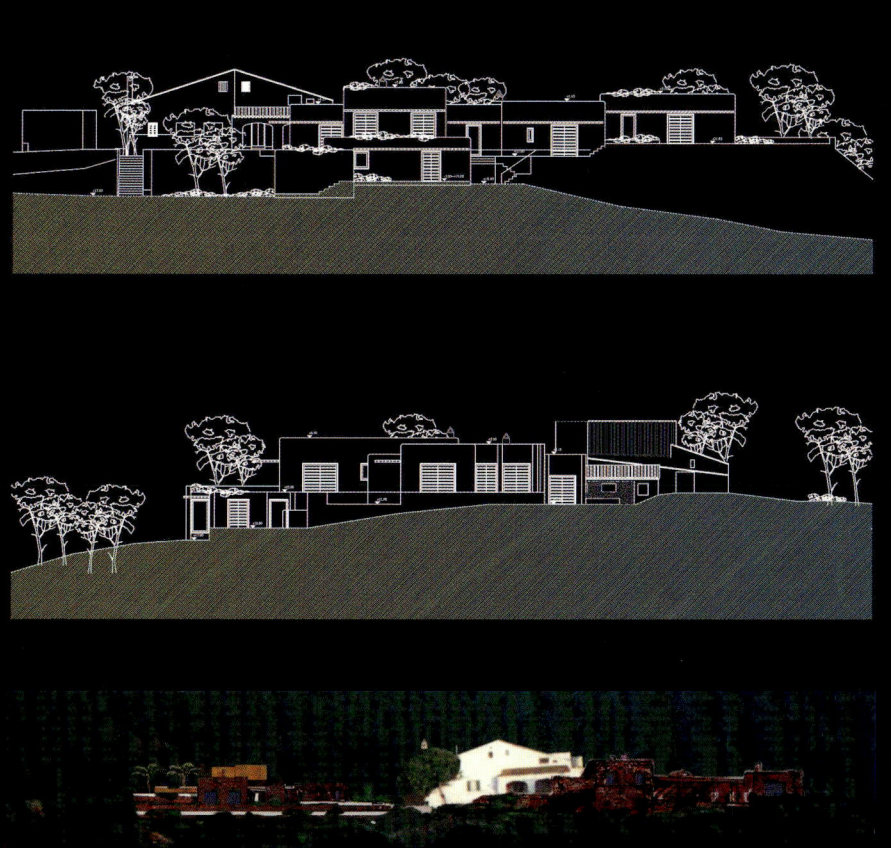
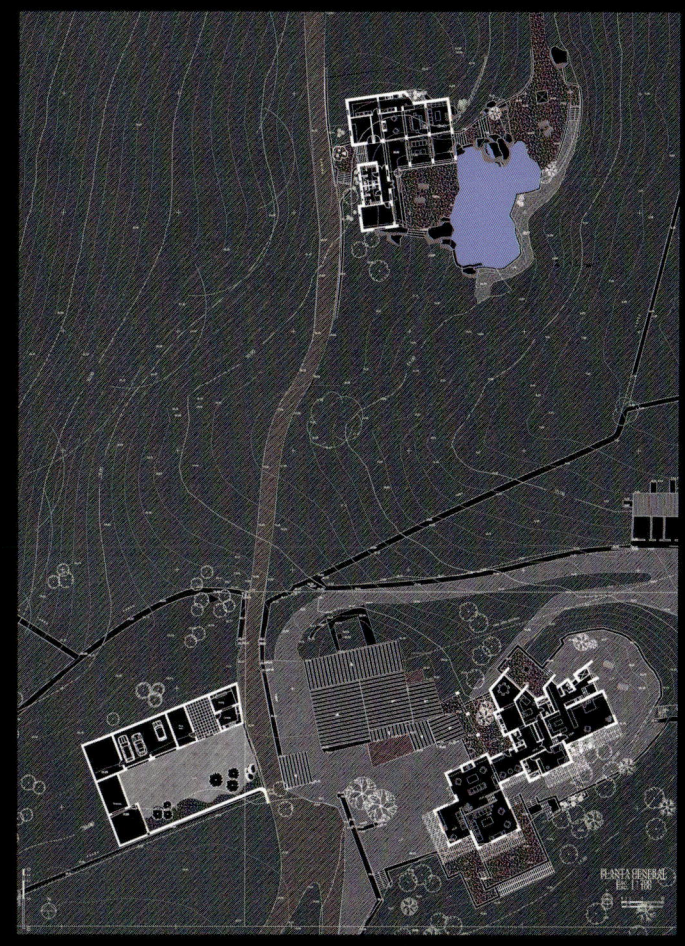

CHILE-CALIFORNIA ROOM FOR BODEGAS TORRES

Vilafranca del Penedès, Spain // 2002

Photos built work

Photomontage

FORUM MONTIJO
Design of the central space

Montijo, Portugal // 2002

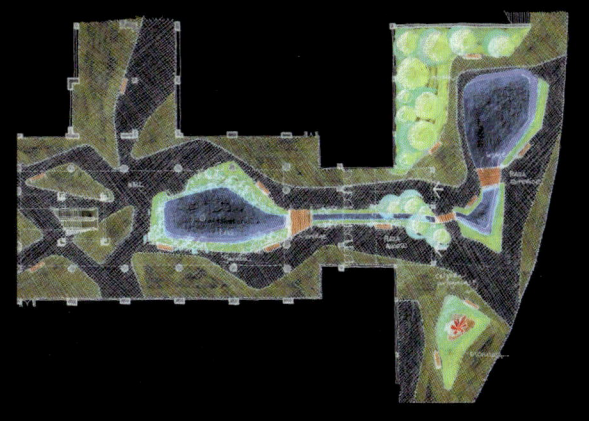
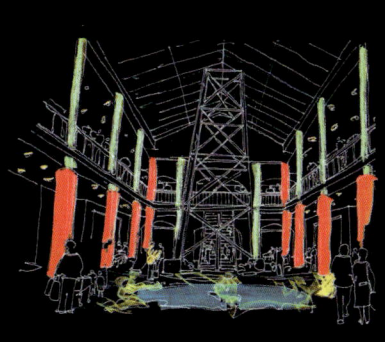
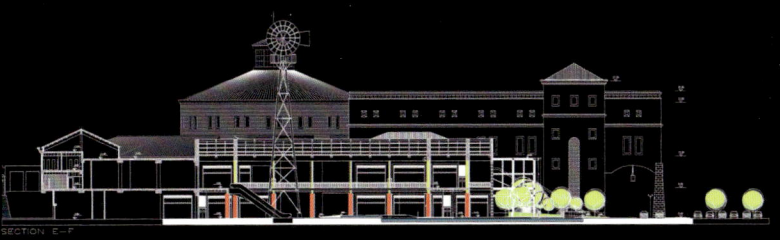

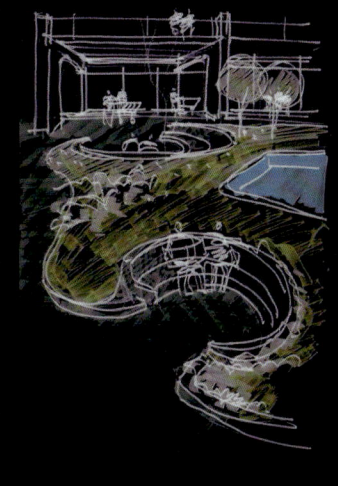
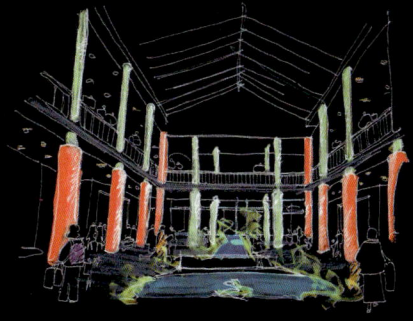
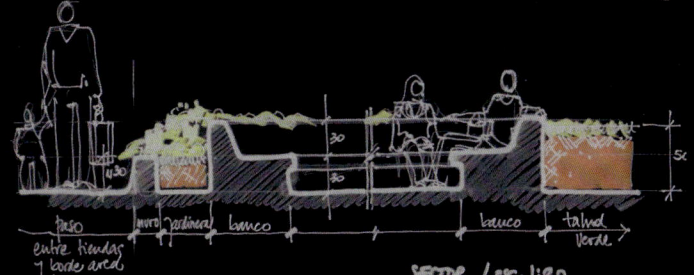

LANDSCAPE IN VALLSOLANA BUSINESS CENTER

Sant Cugat del Vallès, Spain // 2001

Plan, north access

North access

Perspective

PIOLETS HOTEL

Soldeu, Andorra // 2000

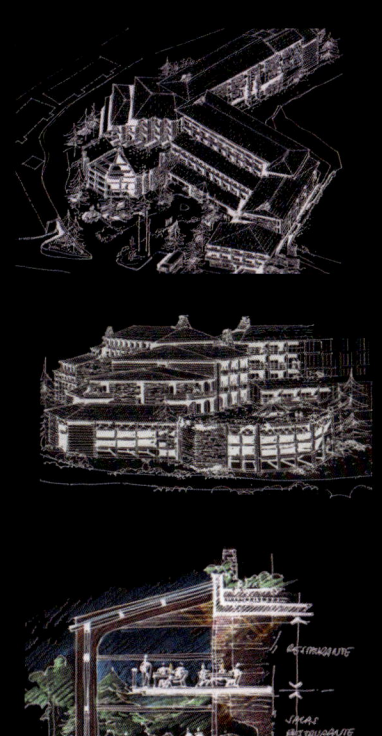

PÉREZ DEL PULGAR HOUSE

Bellaterra, Spain // 2000

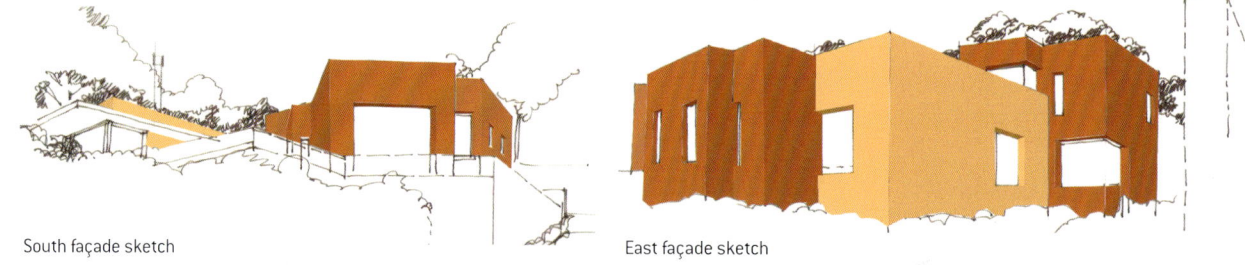

South façade sketch

East façade sketch

GARCÍA NIETO HOUSE

Majorca, Spain // 2003

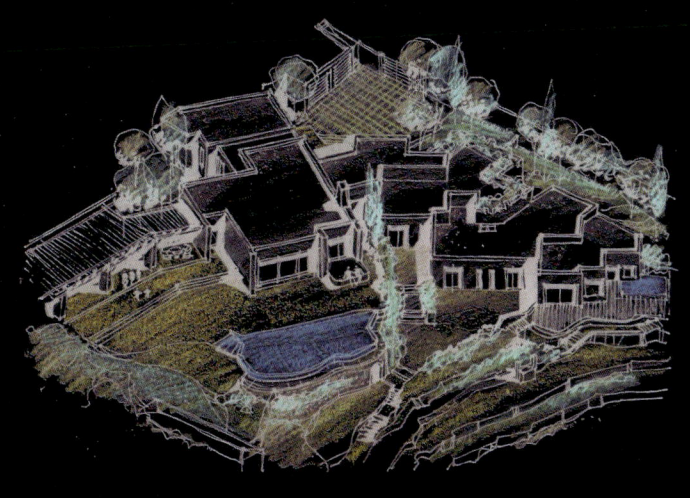
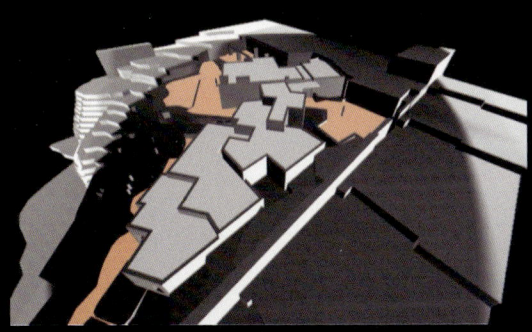

PLANELLS HOUSE

Santa Cristina d'Aro, Spain // 1999

Entrance

FERRER HOUSE

Delta de l'Ebre, Spain // 2006

SÁNCHEZ VICARIO HOUSE

Sitges, Spain // 1999

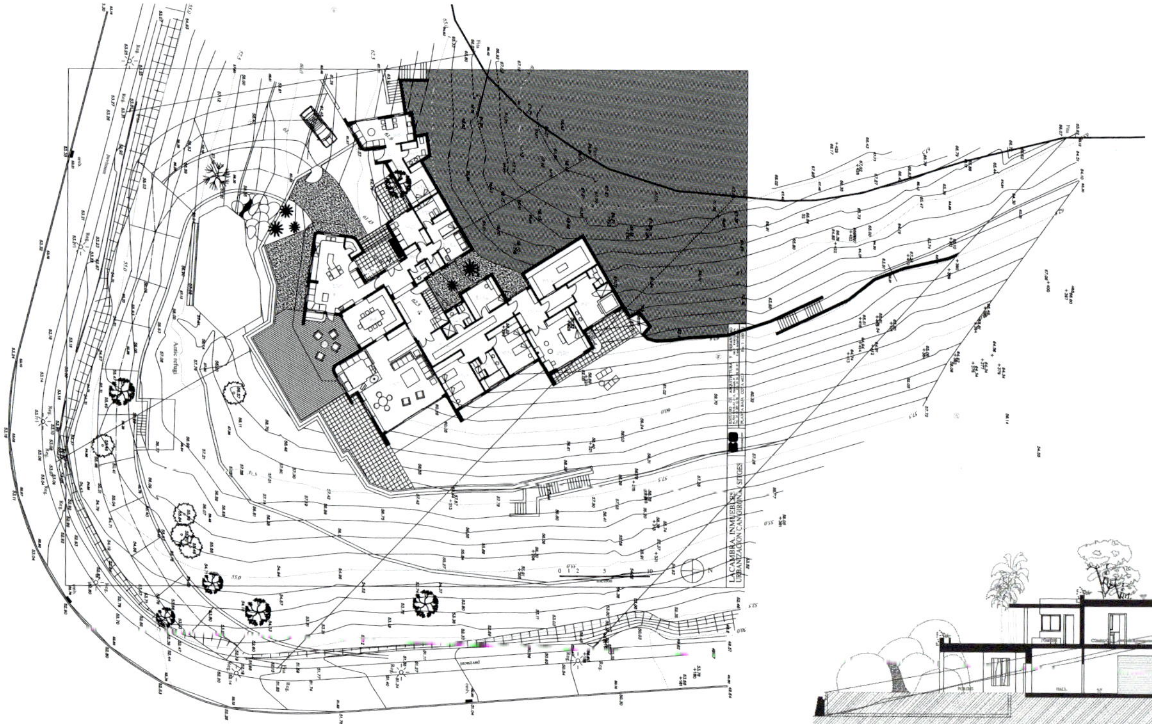

Ground floor

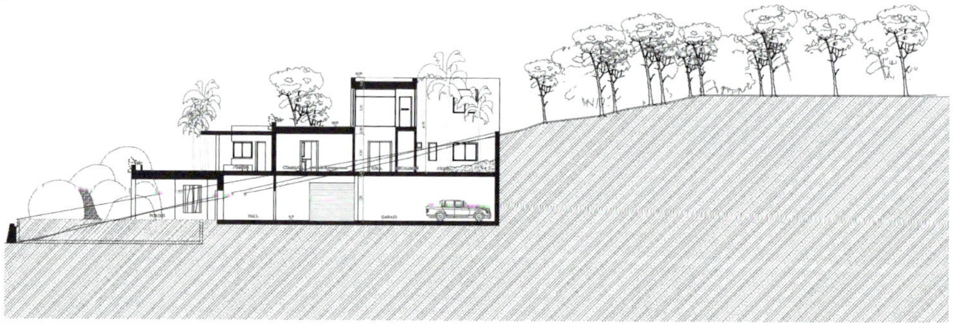

Elevation

Photos of the location

ALMADA FORUM SHOPPING MALL

Almada, Portugal // 1997

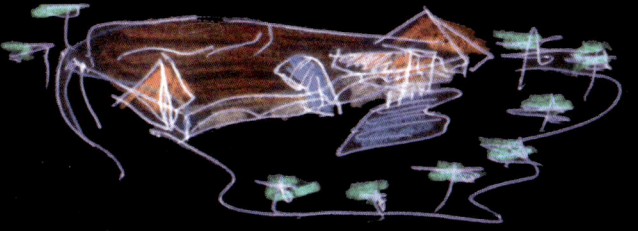

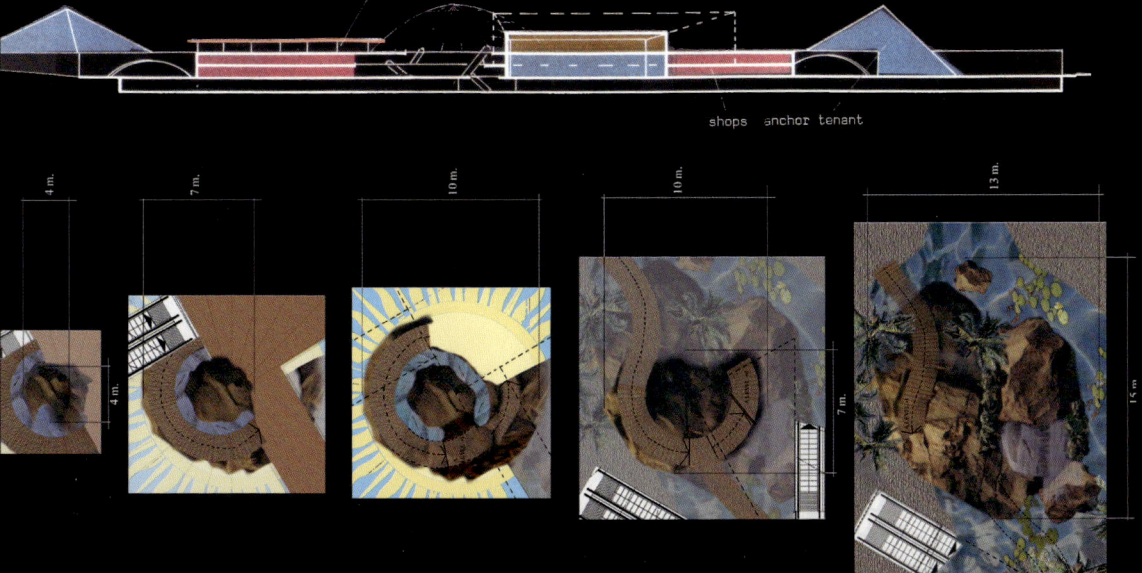

16 Houses in Vallpineda
Sitges, Spain
Village // 1985

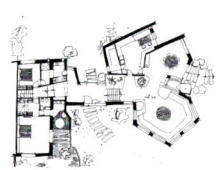
Mora House
Calella de Palafrugell, Spain
Dwelling // 1989
Photos © Eugeni Pons

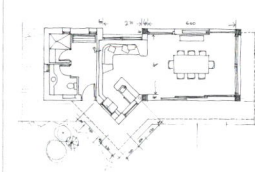
Giró Summer Pavilion
Sitges, Spain
Dwelling // 1995
Photos © Lluís Casals

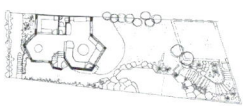
Semel House
Sant Andreu de Llavaneres, Spain
Dwelling // 1985
Photos © Jordi Barba

Green under Green
Barcelona, Spain
Sport facilities // 1986
Photos © courtesy of L35 Arquitectos

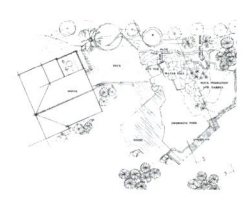
Ryan House
Montana, USA
Dwelling // 1996
Project

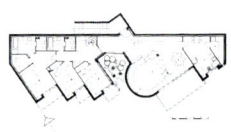
Riera House
Sant Andreu de Llavaneres, Spain
Dwelling // 1986
Photos © Luis Casals
p. 12 down © Jordi Barba
p. 16 right © Jordi Barba

La Isla Verde©
Barcelona, Spain
Residential complexes // 1992
Project

Mora House
Llafranc, Spain
Dwelling // 1997
Photos © Eugeni Pons

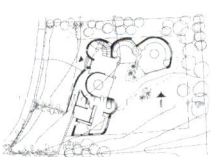
Caralps House
Alella, Spain
Dwelling // 1989
Photos © Emilio Rodríguez

Lord Rothschild Summer Pavilion
Corfu, Greece
Dwelling // 1993
Photos © Eugeni Pons

Los Prados
Oviedo, Spain
Shopping Mall // 1997

House in Olesa
Olesa de Bonesvalls, Spain
Dwelling // 1990

Luxury Resort Hotel in Borobudur
Borobudur, Indonesia
Hotel // 1993
Project

Almada Forum
Almada, Portugal
Shopping Mall // 1997
Project

Monjo House
Minorca, Spain
Dwelling // 1990
Photos © Lluís Casals

Therapeutic-Tourism Complex
Sanillés, Spain
Village // 1994
Project

Tsirigakis House
Mykonos, Greece
Dwelling // 1997
Photos © Eugeni Pons

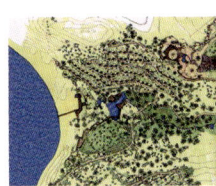
San Basilio Hotel Resort
Baja California, Mexico
Hotel // 1997
Project

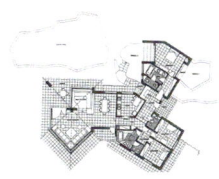
Planells House
Santa Cristina d'Aro, Spain
Dwelling // 1999
Photos © Estudio BC

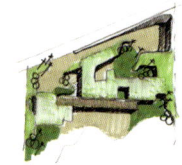
Swarovski House
Tenerife, Spain
Dwelling // 2000
Project

Predio de Sa Fúa
Minorca, Spain
Village // 1998
Photos © Pamela Platt

Sánchez Vicario House
Sitges, Spain
Dwelling // 1999
Project

Zermoma House
Ibiza, Spain
Dwelling // 2000
Photos © Dexter Hodges

Village in Sant Mori
Sant Mori, Spain
Village // 1998
Project

Kantarzopoulos House
Mykonos, Greece
Dwelling // 1999
Project

Zerolo House
Tenerife, Spain
Dwelling // 2000
Project

Swarovski House
Minorca, Spain
Dwelling // 1999
Project

Van Veggel House
Cascais, Portugal
Dwelling // 1999
Photos © Javier Barba

Pérez del Pulgar House
Bellaterra, Spain
Dwelling // 2000
Photos © Michele Curel

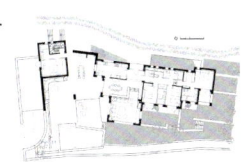
Pi Sunyer House
Cadaqués, Spain
Dwelling // 1999
Photos © Jordi Barba, Pamela Platt

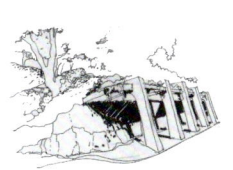
Stag's Leap Wine Cellars
Napa Valley, California, USA
Winery // 1999
Photos courtesy of
Architectural Digest
p. 217 © Daniel D'Agostini

San Blas Valley Resort
Tenerife, Spain
Hotel // 2000

Salvat-Pallejà House
Valldoreix, Spain
Dwelling // 1999
Project

Piolets Hotel
Soldeu, Andorra
Hotel // 2000
Photos courtesy of Ahotels

Deligiannis House
Mykonos, Greece
Dwelling // 2000
Photos © Maria Chatziioanidou

Girod House
Baja California, Mexico
Dwelling // 2000

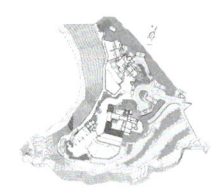

Kokkalis Houses
Mykonos, Greece
Dwelling // 2001
Photos p. 98, 100, 101, 103 (right), 104 © Panagiotis Fotiadis
p. 99, 102, 103 (left), 105 © Julia Klimi

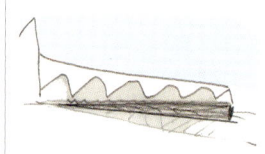

RCD Espanyol Shopping Mall
Cornellà de Llobregat, Spain
Shopping Mall // 2002
Project

Van Veggel House Exterior Areas
Estoril, Portugal
Dwelling // 2000
Photos © Pamela Platt

Economou House
Mykonos, Greece
Dwelling // 2001
Project

Pamekas House
Mykonos, Greece
Dwelling // 2002
Photos © Panagiotis Fotiadis

Huneeus House
Napa Valley, California, USA
Dwelling // 2000
Project

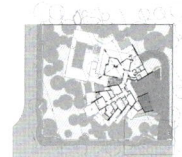

Chalets in Pinhal Velho
Vilamoura, Portugal
Dwelling // 2001
Photos © Vasco Celio

Economou – Vosniades Houses
Skiathos, Greece
Dwelling // 2008
Photos © C. Terzopoulos

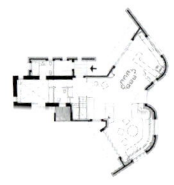

Barba House. Estate Kalandria
Delta de l'Ebre, Spain
Dwelling // 2000
Photo p. 48 (down) © Paisajes Españoles

Forum Montijo
Montijo, Portugal
Shopping Mall // 2002

Village on Paros island
Paros, Greece
Village // 2002
Project

Village, Termal Center and Hotel Cantabria
Ruesga, Spain
Hotel // 2001
Project

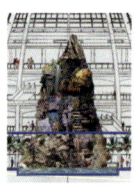

La Roca
Estoril, Portugal
Shopping Mall // 2002

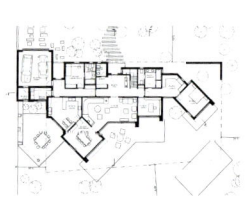

Quinta da Marina
Portugal
Dwelling // 2002
Project

Terzopoulos House
Athens, Greece
Dwelling // 2001
Photos © Julia Klimi

Chile-California Room for Bodegas Torres
Vilafranca del Penedès, Spain
Winery // 2002

Landscape in Vallsolana
Sant Cugat, Spain
Exterior areas // 2001

Colonques House
Minorca, Spain
Dwelling // 2003
Project

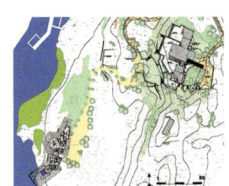
Greenlandia
St. Petersburg, Russia
Dwelling // 2004
Project

Zefkilis House
Athens, Greece
Dwelling // 2006

García Nieto House
Majorca, Spain
Dwelling // 2003
Project

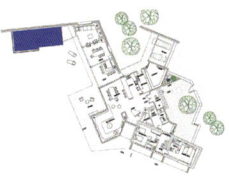
Ferrer House
Delta de l'Ebre, Spain
Dwelling // 2006
Photos © Pamela Platt

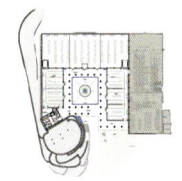
Waltraud cellar for Bodegas Torres
Vilafranca del Penedès, Spain
Winery // 2008
Photos © Jordi Elías
p. 227 © Jordi Barba

18 Houses in Aiguablava
Begur, Spain
Village // 2003
Photos © Jordi Barba

Alice in Wonderland. Kristiansand Performing Arts Center
Kristiansand, Norway
Shopping Mall // 2005

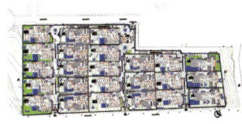
24 Houses in Cala Conta
Ibiza, Spain
Village // 2007

Rallis House
Athens, Greece
Dwelling // 2003
Photos © Julia Klimi

Apartment in St. Petersburg
St. Petersburg, Russia
Dwelling // 2005
Project

Casa Tusquets
Barcelona, Spain
Dwelling // 2009
Photos © Julio Cunill

Stag's Leap Wine Cellars Visitor Center
Napa Valley, California, USA
Winery // 2003
Project

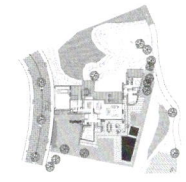
Irbesama House
Baix Empordà, Spain
Dwelling // 2007
Photos © Pamela Platt

HRH Prince Sultan Bin Fahad Red Sea Residence
Jeddah, Saudi Arabia
Village // 2007
Photos © Julio Cunill

Houses in Lia
Mykonos, Greece
Dwelling // 2008
Photos © Maria Chatziioanidou

Condohotel Mojácar for group Med
Mojácar, Spain
Hotel // 2006

12 Luxe Dwellings in Ibiza
Ibiza, Spain
Village // 2008
Project

Jesús Ibiza
Ibiza, Spain
Dwelling // 2008
Project

Dwellings in La Graiera Golf Course
Calafell, Spain
Dwelling // 2009

Paraschis House
Koilada, Greece
Dwelling // 2009

Tree Houses
Ibiza, Spain
Dwelling // 2008
Project

Intervention in Soto de Torres for Bodegas Torres
La Rioja, Spain
Winery // 2009
Photos © Jordi Elías

Houses in Paros
Paros, Greece
Dwelling // 2010

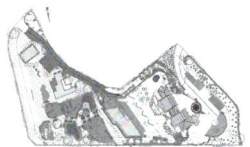
HRH Prince Sultan Bin Fahad residence in Cannes
Cannes, France
Dwelling // 2009

Dunmow House
Athens, Greece
Dwelling // 2009

Club House and spa in Poland
Warsaw, Poland
Club house // 2009

Tree Houses in Agiostephanos
Mykonos, Greece
Dwellings // 2008

House in Agiostephanos
Mykonos, Greece
Dwelling // 2009

Oued Boutique Hotel©
Marrakech, Morocco
Boutique Hotel // 2010

Marina Village Odessa
Odessa, Ukraine
Village // 2008
Project

Black Stone
Athens, Greece
Village // 2009

Jordan House
Alentejo, Portugal
Project // 2010

Club House. Golf La Graiera
Calafell, Spain
Club house // 2009
Project

House in Rodopoli
Athens, Greece
Dwelling // 2009

Casa Sutherland
Sicily, Italy
Project // 2010

Estudio BC

President & CEO of Estudio BC
F. Javier Barba

Study and project director
Arch. Susana Zanón

Estudio BC director
Arch. Gabriel Barba

Interior design director
Arch. Cynthia Fittipaldi

Landscaping director
Bio. Jordi Barba

Project architects
Arch. Margarida Moiteiro
Arch. Susana Procházková
Arch. Eduardo Reguant
Arch. Oriol Casamitjana
Arch. Carlos Gassol
Arch. Joan Sistach
Arch. Antonio Aller

Studio secretary
Véronique Desvenain

A team of architects with a single goal: consistency with the studio's ideas.

Javier Barba is working on developing projects together with his team at Estudio BC, a group of architects of various nationalities that understand and share his vision of architecture. Under the supervision of the project director, Susana Zanón, the studio combines traditional tools – working models and hand drawn sketches – in the early stages of the project (preliminary studies and drafts) with IT in subsequent phases (basic and implementation projects).

The projects start with a traditional design, moving from a quick sketch or summary of the project to an arduous drafting process which often involves redoing the plans until the required form is achieved – the *"recherche patiente"* described by Le Corbusier. Another key element in the design and development of the project is the relationship established with the client, who plays an active role in all phases of the project.

The work in the studio starts with a simple model, based on the understanding of basic rules such as implementation, orientation, the elements representing the local architecture in the region, and those that are already present on the site.

The projects are considered from a comprehensive standpoint: architecture, interior design, landscaping and even the design of specific items. For Estudio BC, visits to the site while the project is in progress are a key point, since this is when the final touches are added that will give each project its own unique, essential character.

Concern for the future, the impact of building in an ever more developed world, along with the need to rationalize the use of resources have driven the work of Estudio BC ever since Javier Barba set up the studio 35 years ago.

BC Estudio de Arquitectura
javbarba@bcarquitectos.com
www.bcarquitectos.com
www.greenarchitecture.com

PUBLICATIONS LIST

"Casa en Ekali". *Architectural Digest*, 2010, August.

"Javier Barba". *Architectural Digest. The World's 20 Greatest Designers of All Time*, Plus: The New AD 100, USA, 2010, January.

La Isla Verde© project at *Il·luminacions. Catalunya visionària* exhibition. Barcelona: CCCB, 2009.

D'Agostini, Daniel; Chapellet, Molly. *Into the Earth. A Wine Cave Renaissance*: Panache Partners, 2009. Cover.

"Mykonos: Distilled (Pamekas House in Mykonos)". *Architectural Digest*, 2008, August. Cover.

"Greek Drama (Kokkalis Houses in Mykonos)". *Architectural Digest*, USA, 2007, August.

"100 new design ideas from the new AD 100". *Architectural Digest*, 2007, January.

Schleifer, Simone K. *Small Eco Houses*: Evergreen, LOFT Publications, 2007. (Project: Riera House).

"Javier Barba". *The Home Magazine*, Bulgary, 2006, November.

Webb, Michael. *Adventurous Wine Architecture*: Images Publishing, 2005. (Project: Stag's Leap Wine Cellars).

"Espaço intemporal". *Casa & Jardim*, Portugal, 2005, September.

"Javier Barba. Arquitectura mayor para un mundo mínimo". *Vía Construcción*, Spain, 2004, August.

Klimi, Julia. *At home in Greece*: Thames & Hudson, 2004.

"PERSONAJES. Javier Barba". *Interclub Magazine*, Spain, 2004, November.

"World's top designers and architects". *Architectural Digest*, USA, 2004, January.

"Javier Barba". *Sovredom Magazine*, Rusia, 2004, October.

"Earth-sheltered House". *La Vanguardia*, Spain, 2004.

Villas &... Spain-Portugal, 2003, June.

"The Green Island". *La Vanguardia*, Spain, 2003, March.

Javier Barba. Member of the Design Awards, AIA. New York, 2003, September.

"Van Veggel, Vervoordt and Barba team to save a Portuguese villa". *Architectural Digest*, 2002, July.

"Javier Barba". *Village, un estilo de vida*, Spain, 2002, spring.

Barba, Javier. *Living with Nature*: Images Publishing Group Pty Ltd, 1999.

"Mykonos motifs. Tsirigakis house". *Architectural Digest*, USA, 1999, January.

"100 Years of Design. (Menorcan House)". *Architectural Digest*, 1999, April.

"La casa enterrada". *Architectural Digest*, 1998, January.

"Calella House". *El Mueble*, Spain, 1995, July.

"The Green Island Project". *El Periódico de Catalunya*, Spain, 1995, July.

"100 Best Architects and Designers". *Architectural Digest*, USA, 1995, September.

"The Green Island". *Barcelona Divina*, 1995.

"Ecological Island". *Villa Olímpica*, 1995, August.

"Un arquitecto propone una isla artificial para Barcelona, La Isla Verde". *La Vanguardia*, Spain, 1995, July.

"Rothschild House". *Architectural Digest*, USA, 1995, October.

Green construction, lecture in Verona, 1995, October.

Green construction, lecture in Vigo, 1995, October.

"Architecture for a Small Planet". *Town & Country*, USA, 1995, September.

"Abrir Vigo al mar". *Faro de Vigo*, Spain, 1995.

"Ecological Architecture". *Atlántico*, Spain, 1995.

"Mar Adentro". *La Vanguardia*, Spain, 1994, March.

"Llavaneras House. Menorcan House". *Metrópolis*, 1992, April.

"Menorcan House". *Casa Vogue*, 1992.

"Spain. Special issue". *Architectural Digest*, pp. 96-101 and cover, 1992, January.

"Menorcan House". *Impermeabilización*, 1992, January.

"Congratulatory letter to the editor". *Architectural Digest*, 1992.

"Menorcan House". *Raum & Wohen*, 1992.

"Alella House". *Diari Avui*, 1992, June.

"Llavaneras House". *Architectural Digest*, 1992.

"Menorcan House". *Casa Oggi*, Italy, 1992, July.

"Earth Sheltered House". *World Residential Design*, 1991.

"Earth Sheltered House". *Green Architecture*, 1991. Ed. Thames and Hudson. Cover.

"Menorcan House". *Houses by the Sea*, 1991.

"Earth Sheltered House". *Country Houses*, 1991.

"House in Menorcan Island". *Green Design*, 1991.

"Earth Sheltered House". *Arquitectura Bioclimática*, 1989.

"Earth Sheltered House". *Project Monitor*, 1989.

"Earth Sheltered House". *Interior Design*, 1989.

"Earth Sheltered House". *Architectural Digest*, 1989, January.

Manual and Technical Guide of Coverings and Ceramic Pavings, 1988.

"Earth Sheltered House". *Architectural Digest*, 1987, January.

"Earth Sheltered House". *Casas Mediterráneas*, 1986.

"Earth Sheltered House". *La Vanguardia*, 1985.